THE INTERNATIONAL

NUMISMATA ORIENTALIA.

THE ADVANCED ARTICLES HAVE BEEN UNDERTAKEN BY THE FOLLOWING CONTRIBUTORS:

DR. H. BLOCHMANN. GENERAL A. CUNNINGHAM. MR. RHYS DAVIDS. DON PASCHUAL DE GAYANGOS. PROFESSOR GREGORIEF. SIR WALTER ELLIOT. M. HENRI LAVOIX. SIR ARTHUR PHAYRE. MR. STANLEY L. POOLE. MR. E. T. ROGERS. M. F. DE SAULCY. M. H. SAUVAIRE. MR. EDWARD THOMAS.

COINS OF THE URTUḲÍ TURKUMÁNS.

BY

STANLEY LANE-POOLE,

CORPUS CHRISTI COLLEGE, OXFORD.

1875.

British Library Cataloguing-in-Publication Data
A catalogue record for this book is available from the
British Library

Stanley Lane-Poole

Stanley Edward Lane-Poole was born on 18th December, 1854 in London, England. He was a British orientalist and archaeologist, and the great-nephew of Edward William Lane – a fellow orientalist, famed for his translation of *One Thousand and One Nights.* His father, Edward Stanley Poole, was also an Arabic scholar, and his mother, Roberta Elizabeth Louisa, was a naturalised German. Sadly, Stanley Lane-Poole's parents died when he was still young, so his great-uncle, Edward William Lane, looked after him and his brother, educating the two boys privately.

Stanley went on to study at Oxford University, starting in 1874, and graduating in modern history in 1877. He only achieved a third class degree however, most likely due to his many extra-curricular activities. The young man was already fascinated by oriental issues, and studied oriental coinage with his uncle, Reginald Stuart Poole, who was keeper of coins at the British Museum. As a result of this, Stanley Lane-Poole worked at the British Museum from 1874 until 1892, cataloguing the institution's Islamic coins. Whilst at the Museum, he completed the *Catalogue of Oriental Coins* (11 vols., 1875–91) and the *Catalogue of Indian Coins* (3 vols., 1884–92). At the same time he also catalogued the *Mohammedan Coins Preserved in the Bodleian Library, Oxford* (1888).

After this experience, Lane-Poole travelled to Egypt in 1883, and spent his time researching Egyptian archaeology, becoming a world-renowned expert in the field. Lane-Poole was later sent, by the 'Department of Science and Art' on more archaeological missions, to Sweden, Russia and

Turkey, in order to investigate Islamic numismatics. Until 1897, he was involved in archaeological research for the Egyptian government, producing a well-received text, the *Arabic Coins Preserved in the Khedival Library at Cairo* (1897).

In his personal life, Lane-Poole married Charlotte Bell Wilson on 15th May, 1879. They had three sons, and a daughter. Lane-Poole returned to Britain in 1897, when he was appointed as Professor of Arabic studies at Trinity College, Dublin University. He remained in this position until 1904 (the year of his retirement), continuing to work unceasingly on his academic studies. During this time, Lane-Poole published numerous books on the life and history of the Muslim world, especially Egypt and India, and edited several works of his great-uncle Lane, including the famous translation of *The Thousand and One Nights* (1883, 1891, 1906).

Lane-Poole's wife died in 1905, after which he lived in retirement at 10 Brompton Square, London. He stayed there until his death, on 29th December, 1931, aged seventy-six. He was cremated at Golders Green crematorium on 1st January 1932.

EDITOR'S NOTE.

It is to be understood that, in this collection of memoirs, authors have the entire credit, and are in the same degree responsible for their own contributions. In the present article, the author has throughout maintained his right of freedom from editorial control. The leading difference, however, has only extended to the severity of the treatment of a subject which the Editor desired to have cast into a more popular form.

A concession has been made in the appended Table of Alphabets to the demands of the contributors to purely Arabic Numismatics, who hesitated to accept the less elaborate Persian system of transliteration suggested by the Editor in the opening Essay: and, at the same time, advantage has been taken of the opportunity to improve some of the minor details of the latter scheme, so as to bring it more into harmony with the newly adapted Arabic compromise, especially in regard to the group of letters ص — ظ, which will now be ranged in more complete unison with the fellow alphabet by the use of single dots below their corresponding Roman letters.

As the retention of the old title of "Marsden" has been misunderstood on the one part, and found to be altogether out of place under the altered conditions of the present publication, the Editor has reverted to the more appropriate term of an *International Edition* of the "Numismata Orientalia."—[E. T.]

The distribution of the sections of the entire work already undertaken comprises the following:

Coins of Southern India	Sir Walter Elliot, late Madras Civil Service.
„ Assam, etc.	Sir Arthur Phayre, late Commissioner in British Burmah.
„ the Indo-Scythians	General A. Cunningham, Archæological Surveyor of India.
„ Ceylon	Mr. T. W. Rhys Davids, late Ceylon Civil Service.
„ the Bengal Sultáns	Dr. Blochmann, the Madrissa, Calcutta.
„ the early Arabico-Byzantine adaptations .	M. de Saulcy, Membre de l'Institut, Paris.
„ the Russo-Tátár Dynasties	Professor Gregorief, St. Petersburg.
„ the Khalifs of Spain, etc.	Don Paschual de Gayangos, Madrid.
„ the Sherifs of Northern Africa	M. Henri Lavoix, Bibliothèque Nationale, Paris.
„ the Fatimites of Egypt	M. Sauvaire, late Consul for France at Cairo.
„ the Túlún Dynasty of Egypt	Mr. E. T. Rogers, Director of Public Instruction, Egypt.
„ the Saljúḳis, Urtuḳis, and Atábegs . . .	Mr. Stanley Lane Poole, Oxford.
„ the Sassanians of Persia	Mr. Edward Thomas, London.

CONTRASTED METHODS OF TRANSLITERATION VARIOUSLY ADVOCATED FOR ARABIC AND PERSIAN, WITH THE SYSTEMS FINALLY ADOPTED FOR THE INTERNATIONAL NUMISMATA ORIENTALIA.

(Cols. 8, 9.)

	1 Sir W. Jones.	2 Mirza Ibrahim	3 Mr. F. Johnson.	4 M. A. Chodzko.	5 Dr. Wright.	6 Dr. Fuerst.	7 Mr. Lane.	8 Persian.	9 Arabic.		1 Sir W. Jones.	2 Mirza Ibrahim.	3 Mr. F. Johnson.	4 M. A. Chodzko.	5 Dr. Wright.	6 Dr. Fuerst.	7 Mr. Lane.	8 Persian.	9 Arabic.
ا	a	a	a	e, a	’			a		ع	ع	a	ع	’a	ʻ		’, ạ	’	’
ب	b	b	b	b	b	b	b	b	b	غ	gh	gh	gh	gh	ġ	ġ	gh	gh	gh
پ	p	p	p	p	p	—	—	p	—	ف	f	f	f	f	f	f	f	f	f
ت	ţ	t	t	t	t	t	t	t	t	ق	ḳ	ck	k	q	ḳ	ḳ	ḳ	ḳ	ḳ
ث	th *or* ṣ	s	s	s	ṯ	t, θ	th	ṡ	th	ك	k̤	k	k	k	k	k	k	k	k
ج	j	j	j	dj	ǵ	ǵ	j	j	j	گ	g	g	g	g	g	—	—	g	
چ	ch	ch	ch	tch	c	—	—	ch		ل	l	l	l	l	l	l	l	l	l
ح	ḥ	h	h	hh	ḥ	ḥ	ḥ	ḥ	ḥ	م	m	m	m	m	m	m	m	m	m
خ	kh	kh	kh	kh	ẖ	ẖ	kh	kh	kh	ن	n	n	n	n	n	n	n	n	n
د	d	d	d	d	d	d	d	d	d	و	v, w	v	v, w	v, oû	w	v, w, û	w	v, w	w
ذ	ż	z	z	z	ḏ	ḏ	dh	ż	đ	ه	h̤	h	h	h, é	h	h	h	h	h
ر	r	r	r	r	r	r	r	r	r	ي	y	y	y	y, î	y	y, i	y	y, i, c	y
ز	z̈	z	z	z	z	z	z	z	z	َ	a	ă	a	e	a, è, e	a *or* e	a *or* e	a, ă	a
ژ	j̈	j	j̈	j	j	—	—	zh	—	ِ	i	ĕ	i	i	i, ì	i *or* y	i	i, e	i
س	s̤	s	s	s	s	s	s	s	s	ُ	u	ū	u	u	u, o, ö	o *or* u	u *or* o	u	u
ش	sh	sh	sh	ch	ś	ś	sh	sh	sh	َا	ā	—	ā	â	ā	—	á	á	á
ص	s̬	s	s	s	ṣ	ṣ	ṣ	ṣ	ṣ	ِى	ī *or* e	—	ī	—	ī	—	ee	í, é	í
ض	ẑ	z	z	z	ḍ	ḍ	ḍ	ẓ	ḍ	ُو	ū *or* o	—	ū	ô *or* ou	ū	—	oo	ú,	ú
ط	ṭ̤	t	t	t	ṭ'	ṭ	ṭ	ṭ	ṭ	َو	{au *or* aw}	—	au	ôou	au, ō	—	ow, ó	au, ó	au
ظ	z̤̈	z	z	z	ẓ	ẓ	ḍh	ẓ	ẓ	َى	ai	—	ay	—	ai, ë	—	ey, ei	ay, ai	ay, ai

The diacritical dots may be omitted at option, but preferentially where the original text accompanies the romanized version.

No. 1.—Persian Grammar. London, 1828. No. 2.—London, 1841.
No. 3.—Persian Dictionary. London, 1852.
No. 4.—Grammaire Persane. Paris, 1852.
No. 5.—Arabic Grammar. London, 1874–75.
No. 6.—Hebrew and Chaldee Lexicon. London, 1867.
No. 7.—Arabic Lexicon. London, 1863–74.
No. 8.—The International Numismata Orientalia—Persian, etc.
No. 9.—*The International Numismata Orientalia*—Arabic.

THE SANSKRIT ALPHABET,

WITH THE CORRESPONDING SYSTEM OF ROMAN EQUIVALENTS ADOPTED IN THE INTERNATIONAL NUMISMATA ORIENTALIA.

Gutturals	क k,	ख kh,	ग g,	घ gh,	ङ ṅ.
Palatals	च ch,	छ chh,	ज j,	झ jh,	ञ ñ.
Cerebrals	ट ṭ,	ठ ṭh,	ड ḍ,	ढ ḍh,	ण ṇ.
Dentals	त t,	थ th,	द d,	ध dh,	न n.
Labials	प p,	फ ph,	ब b,	भ bh,	म m.
Semivowels . . .	य y,	र r,	ल l,	व v,	
Sibilants and Aspirate	श ś,	ष sh,	स s,	ह h.	

Sanskrit vowels.

अ a,	आ á.
इ i,	ई í.
उ u,	ऊ ú.
ऋ ṛi,	ॠ ṛí.
ऌ lṛi,	ॡ lṛí.
ए e,	ऐ ai.
ओ o,	औ au.
अं aṅ,	अः aḥ

AUTHOR'S PREFACE.

THE present Essay is based upon an article on the coins of the Urtuḳí princes which I contributed to the *Numismatic Chronicle* in 1873. The earlier treatise was little more than a catalogue of the series of these coins in the British Museum; but in the present work much has been added from the cabinet of the late Colonel C. Seton Guthrie and from foreign collections described either in published catalogues or in the letters of correspondents abroad. It is needless to say that the whole work has undergone a thorough revision, several errors have been rectified by the acquisition of fresh details, and the historical Introduction has been entirely re-written after a second and more complete examination of the original authorities, and has been supplemented by a comparative table of the contemporary dynasties, including the Kings of Jerusalem and the Emperors of Constantinople; thus bringing the Turkumán highlandmen into relations with names which are more familiar to English readers, and with which these semi-barbarous chieftains had much more to do than is commonly supposed.

The system of transliteration adopted in the present Essay demands some explanation from me. I am unwilling that it should go forth as my own production, for it is not such a system as I should choose for myself. It does not appear to me to answer what I consider a very important end of transliteration,—a true image of the pronunciation. However, it fulfils the at least equally important object of giving an accurate and consistent reproduction of the original orthography. On the whole, in a composite work like the *Numismata Orientalia*, wherein essays by writers of widely differing languages will have a place, the system of transliteration proposed by the Editor is as satisfactory as need be. As I am at present making use of four different systems of transliteration in four different publications, I am inclined to view with equal toleration all systems that are consistent and intelligible.

The mixture of plates, three autotype-photographic, and three copper-plate, is due to the necessity of supplementing the original engravings of Marsden's work by representations of those additions which have been made to the series of numismatic monuments since his time, and to the superiority of photographic over engraved plates. Of the perfect fidelity and clearness of the autotype photographs it is needless to speak; but with regard to the copper-plates it is necessary to say that whilst in many cases the engraver has succeeded in an admirable degree in representing the coins, in some he has been unfortunate. In such cases the student must trust rather to the description than to the engraving.

In the composition of the Essay I have received valuable assistance, in the way of notes upon the earlier article and references to coins with which I was unacquainted, from M. W. Tiesenhausen, of Warschau; Dr. O. Blau, German Consul-General at Odessa; Dr. E. Ritter von Bergmann, Custos of the Imperial Coin-Cabinet at Wien; and from Mr. J. W. Redhouse. I take this opportunity to express to them publicly the thanks which they have already received in private.

STANLEY LANE POOLE.

CORPUS CHRISTI COLLEGE, OXFORD.
October, 1875.

CONTENTS.

	PAGE
Editor's Note	v
Table of Transliteration	vii
Author's Preface	ix
Introduction—§ 1. Images on the Coinage	1
,, § 2. History	2
,, § 3. Mint-places	8
,, § 4. Ornamentation	9
,, § 5. Denomination	9
,, § 6. Weight and Measure	11
,, Table I. Suzerains	11
,, Table II. Contemporary Dynasties	12
,, Table III. Chronological List	14
,, Table IV. Genealogical Tree	14
Coins of the Urtuḳís. I. Of Kayfá	15
,, II. Of Khartapirt	23
,, III. Of Máridín	24
Appendix A. Turkish Names	43
,, B. Palæography	43
,, C. Astrological Types	44
Six Plates.	

CORRECTIONS.

P. 2, line 15, *for* "'Uḳayli," *read* "'Uḳaylí."

P. 4, line 24, *for* "Dháníth," *read* "Ḍáníth."

P. 7, note 5. *For* "The histories can give no information as to the date of Alpí's death, but the coins prove it was 572;" *read*, "The date here given is the traditional one, and I have adopted it as founded probably on some authority with which I am unacquainted. The testimony of Ibn-al-Athír, indeed, is adverse to the date 572; for although he nowhere records the death of Alpí, he mentions his son Ḳuṭb-ad-dín as ruler of Máridín in 569. The coins afford us no help in this matter. On the whole I have thought it better to follow Marsden in adopting the date 572, for which he probably had some authority, in spite of the solitary notice which Ibn-al-Athír opposes to it."

P. 14, note 1, *for* "Ṣálíḥ," *read* "Ṣáliḥ"; and *for* "Abu-l-Fida," *read* "Abu-l-Fidá."

P. 14, line 2 from bottom, *for* "Ḳárá-Arslán," *read* "Ḳará-Arslán."

P. 16, note 1, *dele* comma after "deutscher."

P. 19, no. 15, rev. area, *for* بين *read* بن.

COINS OF THE URTUḲÍ TURKUMÁNS.

INTRODUCTION.

§ 1. Oriental coins seldom possess artistic merits, perhaps least of all the coins of the Urtuḳís, for these have not even the excellence of calligraphy to recommend them. Yet they are far from being the least interesting of their class. The Urtuḳís are among the few Muḥammadan dynasties who ventured to introduce images on their coins. So strong was the stigma attached to representations of living things by the Prophet of Islám, that the most disreputable prince would not venture to engrave his own or any one else's head upon the currency; for had not the Prophet said that for every image of a living thing that a man made he would be required to find a soul on the day of resurrection; and did not the people believe him? Partly from the fear of offending this prejudice, and partly from a natural predilection for whiting sepulchres and combining questionable practices with an unimpeachable orthodoxy, arose the peculiarity of Muḥammadan coins, the absence of images. The Urtuḳí princes were almost the first to despise the popular belief, and to introduce figures on their dies. But they did not, except perhaps in one or two ill-established instances, engrave their own heads, or those of their suzerains; but chose instead the types of the gold issues of the Byzantine emperors, and sometimes of the Seleucidæ, or again of the Sassanian kings. Not only do we find heads of Byzantine emperors and other 'miscreant' rulers, but even Christian religious types, the Virgin, and Christ, with sometimes the inscription 'Emmanuel' in Greek letters. The princes who struck these unorthodox coins could have had no idea of what heresies they were circulating: although, perhaps, after the first step of admitting images at all, they might not stick at the propriety of any particular representation. The issuing of imaged-coins had probably very little to do with either the orthodoxy or the self-exaltation of the issuers,—it was almost a commercial necessity. The Urtuḳí Turkumáns (as well as the contemporary image-coining dynasties) had frequent intercourse with the Greeks and other Christians of the coasts of Asia Minor. To facilitate their monetary exchanges some currency intelligible to both had to be devised. The result was a mixed coinage—Arabic inscriptions with European, generally Byzantine, images. It is true that the Urtuḳí copy represented a widely different metal-value from the Byzantine gold original; but the object was merely to give the Greek merchant some intelligible and distinguishing mark, when he could not read the Arabic inscription.

§ 2. The *history* of the Urtuḳí princes is not eventful. It is precisely the history of all the other petty chiefs of Syria—a series of raids, of guerrillas, of small jealousies, and large crimes. The important part the dynasty played in the wars of the Crusades is the redeeming feature. The influence of the Crusades on Europe has been so great and so many-sided that an interest is imparted to many things which, were it not for their connexion with these wars, might seem uninteresting enough. The annals of these Turkumáns must claim our attention as the history of the most powerful and vigorous enemies the Crusaders encountered before the coming of Ṣaláḥ-ad-dín.[1]

The first mention we find of Urtuḳ, the founder of the dynasty,[2] is when he was serving in the Saljúḳí armies under the generalship of Fakhr-ad-daulah ibn Juhayr. When first he comes before us, in the year of the Flight 477 (A.D. 1084–5), he must have already risen high in the service, for at that time Fakhr-ad-daulah was besieging Ámid, and Urtuḳ possessed sufficient influence to be able to effect the escape of the besieged, the 'Uḳayli Sharaf-ad-daulah Muslim, who had bought the Turkumán's favour by a bribe.[3] Knowing that this connivance, if it took wind, would compromise him in the eyes of his master, Sulṭán Malik Sháh, Urtuḳ changed his service for that of Malik Sháh's brother, Tutush, Sulṭán of Damascus. In 479 Tutush captured Jerusalem, and made Urtuḳ governor in his name,[4] a post which the Turkumán held till his death in 484;[5] and which his sons Sukmán[6] and Íl-Ghází filled till Al-Afḍal, the son of Badr Al-Jamálí, added the Holy City to the dominions of the Fáṭimí Khalífah (489),[7] whereupon Sukmán departed to Ar-Ruhá (Edessa), and Íl-Ghází to Al-'Iráḳ, where he possessed some territory.[8] When Sulṭán Muḥammad came to Ḥulwán in 494, Íl-Ghází entered into his service, and in the following year was made the Sulṭán's *shaḥnah* or agent at Baghdád,[9] the Saljúḳí capital being Iṣbahán. In the same year (495) the other son of Urtuḳ, Sukmán,[10] rendered assistance to Músá when besieged in Al-Mauṣil (Mossoul) by Jakarmish, and received as reward 10,000 dínárs, together with Ḥiṣn Kayfá, a fortress in Diyár-bakr, on the road between Ámid and Jazírat-ibn-'Umar.[11] He had previously possessed, since 488,

[1] My principal authority is Ibn-al-Athír's *Kámil* (to which I refer by the initials I. A.); but I have also made use of Abu-l-Fidá's *Annales*; Ibn-Khallikán's *Biogr. Dict.*, tr. De Slane; *Récueil des Historiens des Croisades*, vol. i.; and, for the Christian side of the Crusade episode, Michaud's *Histoire des Croisades*, 1857 edition.

[2] The Urtuḳís are vulgarly called the Ortokites.

[3] Ibn-al-Athír, x. 86.

[4] Ibn-Khallikán, art. *Ortuk.*

[5] Ibid.

[6] Sukmán is written سكمان on coins, but generally (though not invariably, cf. Ibn-al-Athír, x. 193, note) سقمان in MSS.

[7] I. A. x. 193. Ibn-Khallikán gives 491; and Abu-l-Fidá 489.

[8] His father had formerly possessed Ḥulwán and Al-Jabal, according to Ibn-Khallikán, and they apparently descended to Íl-Ghází. Ḥulwán is a town on the verge of the Sawád (or district of Al-'Iráḳ, extending from Ḥadíthat-al-Mauṣil to 'Abbádán, and from Al-'Udhayb to Ḥulwán, cf. Lane's Lex. voc. سَوَادٌ). Al-Jabal is not so easy to define. It appears to be the province in which are Ar-Rayy and Hamadán, and, in fact, to correspond pretty nearly to Persian 'Iráḳ. See Yáḳút's Mu'jam-al-buldán (Jacut, Geographisches Wörterbuch) s.vv.

[9] I. A. x. 210, 225.

[10] Ibn-al-Athír mentions a third son of Urtuḳ, named Sulaymán. But I am inclined to believe this is a scribe's mistake for Sukmán; for at the end of the passage in which Sulaymán is mentioned, the name of Sukmán is introduced in a very similar manner (I. A. x. 188–90). Two other sons of Urtuḳ are known, 'Abd-Al-Jabbár and Bahrám (see the Genealogical Table).

[11] I. A. x. 234–6. Yáḳút, v. حصن. Kayfá is called Al-Ḥiṣn الحصن on the coins, and sometimes in Ibn-al-Athír.

the town of Sarúj,[1] in Mesopotamia. Soon afterwards Máridín fell into his hands.[2] War had broken out between Sukmán and Kurbúghá, lord of Al-Mauṣil, and the latter had made prisoner a certain Yáḳútí, son of Íl-Ghází, and incarcerated him in the fortress of Máridín, which at that time was attached to the territory of Al-Mauṣil. At the entreaty of the widow of Urtuḳ, however, her grandson was set at liberty, and shortly rewarded his liberator by seizing the fortress in which he had been confined. Dying before long, he was succeeded by his brother 'Alí, who, however, did not keep his possession beyond a very short time. He went to Jakarmish of Al-Mauṣil, leaving Máridín in the charge of a lieutenant, who promptly handed it over to Sukmán.[3]

It is not certain at what time Máridín passed into the hands of Íl-Ghází, the founder of the Máridín branch of the dynasty. Abu-l-Fidá states[4] that when Sukmán died in 498, he was succeeded by his son Ibráhím in Ḥiṣn Kayfá, and that Máridín went to Íl-Ghází; but we cannot infer from his words (وصارت ماردين لأخيه ايلغازى واستقرّت لولده الى يومنا وهى سنة خمس عشر وسبعمائة) that it passed into his possession immediately on the death of his brother. Ibn-Khallikán[5] says that Íl-Ghází became master of Máridín in 501; and he certainly is mentioned by Ibn-al-Athír in 502 as being lord of that fortress.[6] It seems probable that 502 is the true date, for it was in that year that Mujáhid-ad-dín Bahrúz was made *shaḥnah* at Baghḍád[7] in the room of Íl-Ghází, and it would be reasonable to suppose that the latter, on leaving Baghḍád, was presented by his nephew Ibráhím with a fortress, or that he took it whether presented or not. In any case, Máridín must have come into his possession between 498 and 502. Another difficulty is raised by the uncertainty of the date of Ibráhím's death. All that is known is that he succeeded his father in 498, and that in 508 his brother Rukn-ad-daulah Dáwúd was governing Kayfá when Íl-Ghází applied for help against Áḳsunḳur Al-Barsaḳí.[8]

In 511 (A.D. 1117–8) Íl-Ghází obtained a considerable increase to his possessions, by the acquisition of the city of Ḥalab (Aleppo), which the inhabitants, on the death of their governor Lu-lu, voluntarily handed over to the Urtuḳi, who left his son Timurtásh in charge.[9] This Timurtásh was in 515 sent by his father to the court of Sulṭán Maḥmúd, the Saljúḳí, to intercede for the Arab prince Dubays ibn Ṣadaḳah; and the Sulṭán took the opportunity of investing Íl-Ghází with the government of Mayyáfáriḳín,[10] a very important town in Al-Jazírah, which remained in the possession of the Urtuḳís until 580, when Ṣaláḥ-ad-dín (Saladin) took it. In 516 Íl-Ghází died.[11]

Íl-Ghází, well-named 'Star of the Faith,' was certainly the most considerable man of the house of Urtuḳ, and one of the most powerful chiefs of Syria and Mesopotamia. It is true his possessions were not many; but it must be remembered that power at that time meant not territorial sway, but the possession of a few impregnable fortresses, from which the neighbouring country could be scoured.

[1] Abu-l-Fidá, ann. 488 (iii. 298). Cf. I. A. x. 222, from which it may almost be inferred that Sukmán was suzerain of Sarúj, see p. 5, note 4.

[2] Between 495 and 498. The date is fixed by the fact that Jakarmish was ruler of Al-Mauṣil at the time, and that he did not succeed to that government till the death of Kurbúghá in 495; and by Sukmán's death in 498.

[3] The whole story, which is hardly worth enlarging upon here, may be read in Abu-l-Fidá, ann. 498 (iii. 350–3).

[4] *Annales*, iii. 350.

[5] Art. *Urtuk.*

[6] I. A. x. 321. Íl-Ghází seems also to have possessed Niṣíbín at that time.

[7] I. A. x. 330. In Abu-l-Fidá, iii. 360, line 14, توفى should be corrected تولى.

[8] I. A. x. 352–3.

[9] I. A. x. 372.

[10] I. A. x. 418.

[11] I. A. x. 426.

Few fortresses were better fitted for this purpose than Máridín; and to the possession of this stronghold much of Íl-Ghází's reputation must be ascribed. It has already been mentioned that the Urtuḳís took an important part in the wars with the Crusaders. This was chiefly during the period between the First and the Second Crusade, when the Latin kingdom of Jerusalem was in the zenith of its short-lived prosperity. Sukmán distinguished himself in 497 by relieving the Muslims who were besieged in Ḥarrán (Carrhes) by Bohemond of Antioch, Baldwin du Bourg of Edessa, his cousin Joceline de Courtenay, and Tancred of Laodicea. Sukmán headed an army of seven thousand mounted Turkumáns, and joining his forces to those of Jakarmish of Al-Mauṣil defeated the Christian army and took Count Baldwin (called by the Arab writers Al-Ḳummaṣ or Al-Ḳúmaṣ, the *Comes*) and his brother Joceline prisoners.[1]

But Íl-Ghází had very much more to do with the Crusaders than Sukmán. Michaud characterizes him as 'le plus farouche des guerriers d'Islamisme'; and he was certainly the most formidable enemy the Crusaders encountered before Ṣaláḥ ad dín arose and drove them before him. The greater part of Íl-Ghází's life was spent in fighting with the infidels; but his principal victory was in 513, when the Crusaders were besieging Ḥalab.[2] It will be remembered that in 511 the Ḥalabís voluntarily accepted the Urtuḳí as their master. But when they found the city surrounded by the armies of the Franks, instead of appealing to their sovereign, they asked help from Baghdád: but none was given. In this emergency, Íl-Ghází, hearing of their distress, marched from Máridín at the head of three thousand horse and nine thousand foot. On his approach the Crusaders beat a retreat to a strong position on a hill called 'Ifrín, where they did not expect the Turkumán would venture to attack them. Nothing daunted, Íl-Ghází led his men up the hill and gained a signal victory. Among the slain was Roger, Regent of Antioch during the minority of Bohemond II.[3] Soon afterwards, however, Baldwin II. (du Bourg), King of Jerusalem, retaliated by obtaining a victory over Íl-Ghází and Dubays at Dhánith-al-baḳl.

When Íl-Ghází died,[4] his elder son Sulaymán succeeded to the government of Mayyáfáriḳín,

[1] I. A. x. 256–7. Michaud thus describes the battle, or rather the surprise:—'Au printemps de l'année 1104, Bohémond avec ses chevaliers, Tancrède alors seigneur de Laodicée et d'Apamée, Baudouin du Bourg, comte d'Édesse ou Roha, et son cousin Joscelin de Courtenai, maître de Turbessel, se réunirent pour passer l'Euphrate et pour mettre le siége devant la ville de Charan ou Carrhes, occupée par les infidèles. . . . Quand les princes chrétiens arrivèrent devant la ville, ils la trouvèrent en proie à la disette et presque sans moyens de défense. Les habitants avaient envoyé solliciter des secours à Maridin, à Mossoul, et chez tous les peuples musulmans de le Mésopotamie. Après quelques semaines de siége, ayant perdu l'espoir d'être secourus, ils résolurent d'abandonner la place et proposèrent une capitulation, qui fut acceptée. Tandis qu'on jurait de part et d'autre d'exécuter fidèlement les conditions du traité, il s'éleva une vive contestation entre le comte d'Édesse et le prince d'Antioche, pour savoir quel drapeau flotterait sur les murs de la cité. L'armée victorieuse attendait, pour entrer dans la ville, que cette contestation fût terminée; mais Dieu voulut punir le fol orgueil des princes, et leur retira la victoire qu'il leur avait envoyée. Baudouin et Bohémond se disputaient encore la ville conquise, lorsque tout à coup on aperçut sur les hauteurs voisines une armée musulmane s'avançant en ordre de bataille et les enseignes déployées. C'étaient les Turcs de Maridin et de Mossoul qui venaient au secours de la ville assiégée. A leur approche, les chrétiens, frappés de stupeur, ne songent plus qu'à fuir. En vain les chefs cherchèrent à ranimer leurs soldats, en vain l'évêque d'Édesse, parcourant les rangs, voulut relever les courages abattus: dès la première attaque, l'armée de la croix fut dispersée; Baudouin du Bourg et son cousin Joscelin furent faits prisonniers; Bohémond et Tancrède échappèrent presque seuls à la poursuite du vainqueur.'—i. 300, 301.

[2] I. A. x. 389–90.

[3] Michaud (i. 317, 318) gives a somewhat different account of the battle, omitting all mention of the provocation offered by the Crusaders in besieging Ḥalab, and attributing the defeat partly to a sand-storm. This explanation seems, *εἰ καὶ γελοιότερον εἰπεῖν*, to put the cart before the horse. It was doubtless the vigorous action of the feet of the flying Crusaders that stirred up the sand, not the sand that caused the flight.

[4] 'Dieu permit alors que le redoutable chef des Turcomans, Ylgazy, terminât sa carrière, frappé par une mort subite et violente.'—Michaud, i. 319. But he does not give any authority for the 'subite et violente' nature of the death.

Timurtásh to that of Máridín, and their cousin Sulaymán ibn 'Abd-Al-Jabbár ibn Urtuḳ to that of Ḥalab.¹ This Sulaymán ibn 'Abd-Al-Jabbár had been made governor of Ḥalab by Îl-Ghází in 515, when his son Sulaymán (who afterwards succeeded to the government of Mayyáfáriḳín) had endeavoured to stir up a revolt in Ḥalab against his father.²

We have now to notice another member of the family of Urtuḳ, the true successor of Îl-Ghází in his wars against the Crusaders.³ This was Balak, son of Bahrám, and grandson of Urtuḳ. He first comes into notice in 497 (A.D. 1103–4), when he possessed himself of 'Ánah and Al-Ḥadíthah, in place of Sarúj, which had been wrested from him in 494 by the Crusaders.⁴ He again appears in 515 (A.D. 1121–2) as having made prisoner Joceline de Courtenay, Count of Edessa,⁵ and his brother Galeran, and shut them up in a fortress called by the Crusaders Quart-Pierre, by the Muslims Khartapirt, in Diyár-bakr.⁶ Baldwin, King of Jerusalem, marching to relieve Kar-kar, which was being besieged by Balak, was defeated and made prisoner, and he too was confined in Khartapirt, where Joceline and Galeran were already incarcerated.⁷ 'Les vieilles chroniques ont célébré la valeur héroïque de cinquante Arméniens qui se dévouèrent pour la délivrance des princes chrétiens. Après avoir invoqué la protection du Tout-Puissant, ils s'introduisirent dans la forteresse de *Quart-Pierre*, déguisés, selon quelques historiens, en marchands, selon d'autres, en moines. A peine entrés dans la citadelle, cette élite de braves, quittant leur déguisement et montrant leurs armes, massacrèrent la garnison musulmane, et rendirent la liberté aux illustres prisonniers. Ce château, dont les chrétiens venaient ainsi de se rendre maîtres, renfermait des vivres en abondance et toutes sortes de munitions de guerre. Balac y avait laissé ses trésors, ses femmes et les plus précieuses dépouilles des pays dévastés par ses armes. Les guerriers chrétiens se réjouirent d'abord du succès de leur entreprise; mais bientôt les Turcs du voisinage se réunirent en foule et vinrent assiéger la forteresse où flottait l'étendard du Christ. Le sultan Balac, qui, selon les récits du temps, avait été averti en songe des projets formés contre lui, rassemble son armée et jure d'exterminer Baudouin, Joscelin et leurs liberateurs. Ceux-ci ne pouvaient résister longtemps à toutes les forces réunies des Turcs, s'ils n'étaient secourus par leurs frères les chrétiens. On décide alors que Joscelin sortira de la forteresse et qu'il ira dans les villes chrétiennes implorer le secours des barons et des chevaliers. Joscelin part aussitôt, après avoir fait le serment qu'il laissera croître sa barbe et qu'il ne boira point de vin jusqu'à ce qu'il ait rempli sa mission périlleuse ; il s'échappe à travers la multitude ménaçante des musulmans, passe l'Euphrates, porté sur deux outres de peau de chèvre, et, traversant toute la Syrie, arrive enfin à Jérusalem, où il dépose dans l'église du Saint-Sépulchre les chaînes qu'il avait portées chez les Turcs, et raconte en gémissant les aventures et les périls de Baudouin et de ses compagnons. A sa voix,

---

¹ I. A. x. 426.
² I. A. x. 417, 418.
³ 'Neveu et successeur d'Ylgazy, . . . semblable au lion de l'Écriture, qui rôde sans cesse pour chercher sa proie.'— Michaud, i. 319.
⁴ I. A. x. 252. Cf. x. 222. Perhaps Balak governed in Sukmân's name. Cf. p. 3.
⁵ Joceline had been the chief advocate of the claims of Baldwin du Bourg, Count of Edessa, to the throne of Jerusalem, left vacant by the death of Baldwin I., and was presented with the principality of Edessa by Baldwin II. in gratitude for his friendly services. He was also master of Sarúj, formerly the possession of Balak, who owed him a grudge for the loss of the place. Joceline had before been made prisoner by Sukmân, and had been sent to Baghdád, where he remained five years.
⁶ I. A. x. 418, 419.   ⁷ I. A. x. 433.

un grand nombre de chevaliers et de guerriers chrétiens jurent de marcher à la délivrance de leur monarque captif. Joscelin se met à la tête; il s'avançait vers l'Euphrate; les plus braves de guerriers d'Édesse et d'Antioche avaient réjoint ses drapeaux, lorsqu'on apprit que le farouche Balac venait de rentrer de force dans le château de Quart-Pierre. Après le départ de Joscelin, Baudouin, Galéran, et les cinquante guerriers d'Arménie avaient soutenu longtemps les attaques des musulmans; mais les fondements du château ayant été minés, les guerriers chrétiens se trouvèrent tout à coup au milieu des ruines. Balac, laissant la vie au roi de Jérusalem, l'avait fait conduire dans la forteresse de Charan.[1] Les braves Arméniens étaient morts au milieu des supplices, et la palme du martyre avaient été le prix de leur dévouement. Quand Joscelin et les guerriers qui le suivaient apprirent ces tristes nouvelles, ils perdirent tout espoir d'exécuter leur projet, et retournèrent les uns à Édesse et à Antioche, les autres à Jérusalem, désolés de n'avoir pu donner leur vie pour la liberté d'un prince chrétien.'[2]

Balak's career was brilliant but short. Whilst besieging Manbij in 518, he fell by the hand of that very Joceline whom he had formerly imprisoned.[3] His head was carried in triumph before the walls of Tyre, which was then besieged by the Crusaders. His cousin Timurtásh succeeded him in his possessions, of which the most important was the city of Ḥalab, which Balak had taken from Badr-ad-daulah Sulaymán ibn 'Abd-Al-Jabbár in 517,[4] considering him incapable of protecting it from the Franks. Ḥalab did not long continue in the possession of the Urtuḳís. Timurtásh returned to his favourite heights of Diyár-bakr; and Ḥalab, thus left to take care of itself, when besieged not long afterwards by the Crusaders, opened its gates to Al-Barsaḳí, and never again owned a member of the house of Urtuḳ for its master.

Ḥusám-ad-dín Timurtásh died in 547 (A.D. 1152–3), prince of Máridín and Mayyáfáriḳín, as Ibn-al-Athír expressly states.[5] It will be remembered that when Íl-Ghází died, his elder son Sulaymán succeeded him in Mayyáfáriḳín. At what time, then, did the town pass into the hands of Timurtásh? The only clue is supplied by a record by Ibn-al-Athír of the death of a certain Shams-ad-daulah, son of Íl-Ghází, in 518.[6] As the death of Sulaymán is nowhere mentioned, one cannot help conjecturing that this Shams-ad-daulah was none other than he.[7] Timurtásh was succeeded by his son Najm-ad-dín Alpí.

Meanwhile, Dáwúd of Kayfá was gathered to his fathers, and Ḳará-Arslán, his son, ruled in his stead. The death of Dáwúd must have taken place about 543; for he is mentioned by Ibn-al-Athír in 541,[8] and in 542 the "lord of Al-Ḥiṣn" صاحب الحصن is spoken of,[9] but his name is not given, from which we may infer that it was still the name which had been referred to before; and in 544 mention is made of the new ruler Ḳará-Arslán.[10] Fakhr-ad-dín Ḳará-Arslán governed Kayfá and the greater part of Diyár-bakr[11] till the year 570, when he died; and his son Muḥammad ruled after him.[12]

[1] Of which he had just made himself master, 517.—I. A. x. 433.
[2] Michaud, i. 320, 321.
[3] Michaud, i. 325. I. A. x. 436.
[4] I. A. x. 431. He did not, however, put Sulaymán to death; for this prince is mentioned again by Ibn-al-Athír in 523, as mixing in the political affairs of Ḥalab, of which 'Imád-ad-dín Zangí had then made himself master (x. 457).
[5] I. A. xi. 115.
[6] I. A. x. 441.
[7] I have treated the two as identical in the Genealogical Table.
[8] I. A. xi. 73.
[9] I. A. xi. 81.
[10] I. A. xi. 92.
[11] اكثر ديار بكر, I. A. xi. 217.
[12] Ibn-al-Athír, xi. 207, gives the date 562, but the coins prove it to have been 570, or perhaps 571.

Not long after, the Urtuḳís heard the first whirr of the machine that was eventually to grind them to powder. It came about in this way. The town of Al-Bírah on the Euphrates (not that near Aleppo) was being besieged by 'Imád-ad-dín Zangí in 539, but matters needed his presence at Al-Mauṣil, and Zangí abandoned the siege. The 'Franks' who held the town knew well that if Zangí returned, they could not hold out against him; so, making a virtue of a necessity, they handed the place over to Najm-ad-dín Alpí, who is called by Ibn-al-Athír in this instance 'lord of Al-Ḥiṣn' صاحب الحصن, although Timurtásh was still alive.[1] Some time before 565,[2] Al-Bírah was in the possession of Shiháb-ad-dín, a son of Íl-Ghází, who had distinguished himself under the great Núr-ad-dín (Nourredin) of Ḥalab in war with the Crusaders. The time of Shiháb-ad-dín's death is not accurately known, but his son, who appears to be nameless,[3] was governing Al-Bírah in 577 (A.D. 1181–2),[4] when his kinsman Ḳuṭb-ad-dín Íl-Ghází II. of Máridín, who had come to the throne on the death of his father Najm-ad-dín Alpí in 572,[5] laid siege to the town. Shiháb-ad-dín's son, finding himself deserted by his liege-lord, the Atábég of Al-Mauṣil, called in the help of the world-famous *Ṣaláḥ-ad-dín*, who summarily ordered Ḳuṭb-ad-dín back to his own territory, an order with which the Urtuḳí thought it prudent not to quarrel. It was thus that the first contact between the houses of Urtuḳ and Ayyúb came about.

The princes of Kayfá were more far-sighted than their kinsmen of Máridín, and took all pains to keep on good terms with the Ayyúbís. When Ṣaláḥ-ad-dín came northward in 578, Núr-ad-dín of Kayfá was quick to pay homage and to assist in the siege of Al-Mauṣil. The politic prince was rewarded with the important town of Ámid, which the Ayyúbí gave him in the following year (579).[6] Núr-ad-dín enjoyed his new possession for two years, and then died and left it to his son Ḳuṭb-ad-dín Sukmán (581).[7]

Here I must notice a small branch of the Kayfá dynasty,[8] which came into existence on the death of Núr-ad-dín in 581. This prince had a brother, 'Imád-ad-dín, who was at the camp of Ṣaláḥ-ad-dín (again lying before Al-Mauṣil) at the time of Núr-ad-dín's death. In the hope of succeeding to his brother's power, 'Imád-ad-dín immediately set off to Kayfá; but finding his nephew in full possession, he consoled himself with the fortress of Khartapirt,[9] which it will be remembered belonged formerly to Balak.[10] It is not certain when 'Imád-ad-dín died; but in 601 his son Niẓám-ad-dín Abú-Bakr is recorded to have been besieged unsuccessfully by Maḥmúd of Kayfá and Ámid.[11] Khartapirt remained in the family of 'Imád-ad-dín till 620,[12] when it seems to have passed into the hands of the Máridín dynasty; for when it was taken in 631 by Kay-Ḳubád, the Saljúḳí Sulṭán of Ar-Rúm, the governor was of the family of the Urtuḳís of Máridín.[13]

1 I. A. xi. 67, 68. Cf. xi. 115.

2 Ibn-al-Athír, ann. 565, xi. 232, speaks of Shiháb-ad-dín Ilyás ibn Íl-Ghází possessing the fortress of Al-Bírah.

3 Some MSS. of Ibn-al-Athír give اسمه followed by a blank. xi. 313, note.

4 I. A. xi. 313, 314.

5 The histories can give no information as to the date of Alpí's death, but the coins prove it was 572.

6 I. A. xi. 324.

7 I. A. xi. 339.

8 This, the *Khartapirt branch* of the dynasty, was entirely unknown to numismatists before the publication of my Essay on the Urtuḳís in the *Numismatic Chronicle*, vol. viii. N.S. 1873. The coins struck by Abú-bakr of Khartapirt have always been a puzzle to numismatists, and have given rise to the wildest misreadings.

9 I. A. xi. 339.

10 p. 5.

11 I. A. xii. 132.

12 I. A. xi. 339.

13 Abu-l-Fidá, iv. 404. وكان من الارتقية قرايب اصحاب ماردين

The death of Ḳuṭb-ad-dín I'l-Ghází II. in 580[1] was followed by the loss of Mayyáfáriḳín, which the Sháh-Arman took, and which subsequently was given up to Ṣaláḥ-ad-dín. Ḳuṭb-ad-dín was succeeded by his son Yúluḳ- (or Búluḳ- or Búlúḳ-) Arslán;[2] whose brother Urtuḳ-Arslán next followed, some time between the years 596 and 598, as the coins prove.[3] In 599 Al-'A'dil, the brother of Ṣaláḥ-ad-dín, gave orders to Al-Ashraf to besiege Máridín; but by the mediation of Aẓ-Ẓáhir Ghází of Ḥalab an accommodation was arrived at. Urtuḳ-Arslán agreed to insert the name of Al-'A'dil in the Khuṭbah and Sikkah, or public prayer and coinage, and to pay a fine of 150,000 dínárs.[4] This is well borne out by the coins. A coin of 599 (which must refer to the early part of the year)[5] bears the name of Aẓ-Ẓáhir as well as that of Urtuḳ-Arslán, thus showing the friendly relations which subsisted between the two. Further, another coin of 599 (which must have been struck rather later in the year) bears the name of Al-'A'dil as suzerain, thus fulfilling one of the two stipulations of the treaty. After this the Urtuḳís of Máridín withdrew from the affairs of Syria, and kept within the limits of their mountain fastness. Abu-l-Fidá continues the list of princes down to his own time (715 = A.D. 1315–6) when an Urtuḳí prince was still ruling in Máridín;[6] and, for aught I know, the family may still have its representative there.

The Kayfá branch came to an end in 629 (A.D. 1231–2). Sukmán II. was killed in 597, by falling from a housetop.[7] He had himself appointed as his successor a Mamlúk named Ayás, to the exclusion of his own brother Maḥmúd; but the amírs of A'mid invited Maḥmúd to come and take possession, and he did not decline.[8] Maḥmúd died in 619, and his son Al-Malik Al-Mas'úd Maudúd succeeded.[9] But in 629 Al-Kámil the Ayyúbí marched upon A'mid, and took it together with its dependencies,[10] which had been diminished by the inroads of the Sulṭán of Ar-Rúm. Maudúd was imprisoned until the death of Al-Kámil, when he escaped (635), and took refuge with Al-Muẓaffar of Ḥamáh, and eventually died at the hands of the Tatar invaders.[11] So ends the history of the Urtuḳís.

§ 3. Five mint-names are found on Urtuḳí coins.

Urtuḳís of Ḥiṣn Kayfá.	Urtuḳís of Máridín.
الحِصْن *The Fortress* (sc. Kayfá).	مَارِدِين *Máridín.*
آمِد *Ámid.*	دُنَيْسِر *Dunaysir.*
	كيفا *Kayfá.*

No mint-name has as yet been deciphered on the few coins at present extant of the Urtuḳís of Khartapirt.

It is difficult to explain the occurrence of the name *Kayfá* on silver coins of Urtuḳ-Arslán.

[1] I. A. xi. 335.

[2] Written in Ibn-al-Athír بولق without diacritical points to the first letter.

[3] Ibn-al-Athír mentions Yúluḳ-Arslán being alive when Máridín was unsuccessfully besieged by Al-'A'dil in 594–5.—xii. 98.

[4] I. A. xii. 117.

[5] It was in the first month (Al-Muḥarram) that Al-'A'dil gave orders for the siege of Máridín.—I. A. xii. 117.

[6] Abu-l-Fidá, v. 295.

[7] I. A. xii. 112.

[8] *Ibid.*

[9] I. A. xii. 260.

[10] Abu-l-Fidá, iv. 393. وسلم امد وبلادها اليه ومن جملة معاقلها حصن كيفا; but see p. 9 with regard to Kayfá.

[11] Abu-l-Fidá, iv. 393.

There can be no doubt whatever about the reading of the name. The letters بكيفة are perfectly clear, and that is sufficient to establish the reading, although the last letter seems to resemble a ة rather than an ا; it may perhaps be the beginning of the final letter ى, which ends the word according to the Ḳámús orthography. But how did Kayfá come into the possession of the princes of Máridín? Abu-l-Fidá tells us that in 629 Al-Kámil took A'mid and its dependencies, among which was Ḥiṣn Kayfá.[1] His son Aṣ-Ṣáliḥ was left in possession of A'mid, and (we infer from Abu-l-Fidá's account) of Ḥiṣn Kayfá also. But this coin shows that Kayfá belonged to the prince of Máridín in 628, the year before the taking of A'mid. Either, then, we must suppose Maudúd of A'mid to have recovered Kayfá from his kinsman before Al-Kámil's arrival; or else that Abu-l-Fidá, accustomed to regard Kayfá and A'mid as belonging to the same master, erroneously classed Kayfá among the dependencies of A'mid when the latter was taken by Al-Kámil. With our present data it is impossible to decide the question.

Three other mints have been wrongly attributed to the Urtuḳí princes:—حَمَاة *Ḥamáh*, دِيَارْبَكْر *Diyár-bakr*, and مَيَّافَارِقِين *Mayyáfáriḳín*. Ḥamáh is a misreading due to imperfect specimens. Dr. Blau[2] inferred from the letters اة . . . that the mint was حماة, when in fact the letters were . . ار . .; and from other specimens I proved the mint to be ماردين *Máridín*.[3] At the time Dr. Blau's coin was struck (545), the Ayyúbí prince Al-Manṣúr Muḥammad (uncle of the historian Abu-l-Fidá) was ruling Ḥamáh, and his name would certainly appear on any coin struck there. By Diyár-bakr I believe Soret simply to have meant a town in Diyár-bakr, namely Kayfá, or A'mid, or Máridín, or Dunaysir. Mayyáfáriḳín (ميعفرقين or مافرقين *sic*!!) is a magnificent blunder for the words ملعون من of the damnatory formula ملعون من يعيّره.

§ 4. The principal ornaments used on the coins of the Urtuḳís are the Urtuḳí damghah or badge (⩡); an ornament which I have called 'fleuron' (⟗); an inverted chevron, like the orthographical sign *ihmál* or *muhmilah* (V); a semicircle (◡); and points, singly or in groups. Diacritical points are used sparingly on the coins, but they are recorded when they occur. There is generally a centre-point, where the point of one limb of the compasses was placed when the marginal circles were being scored. Near the edge of the coin is generally a circle or several circles, usually of dots.

§ 5. To what denomination the Urtuḳí copper coins are to be referred is not an easy question to answer. Almost all Muḥammadan coins up to the time of these princes belonged to one of the three classes—*dinár* (gold), *dirham* (silver), *fals* (copper). It would be natural to attribute the large copper issues of the Urtuḳís (and some of the contemporary dynasties) to the class of *fals*; but this is clearly forbidden by the fact that some of these copper coins are inscribed with the words

هذا الدّرهم ملعون من يعيّره

Cursed be he who tests this *dirham*.[4]

[1] See p. 8, note 10.

[2] *Zeitschrift der deutsch. morgenländ. Gesellschaft*, xi. 453, no. 24.

[3] *Numismatic Chronicle*, xiii. p. 280.

[4] Dr. Karabacek's rendering of the word يعيّر (*einen Schimpf anthut*) is strictly accurate; and it is quite possible that in this formula the Urtuḳí prince intended to forestall any imprecations that might be launched against his copper coinage, by taking the initiative himself in cursing. I think, however, that a more probable rendering is that of *testing* the coin. In Lane's Arabic Lexicon, part v. art. عير, we find the very expression that occurs

This inscription, which occurs on several plain copper coins, suggested the theory which Dr. Joseph Karabacek has ably put forth in the *Numismatische Zeitschrift* of Wien,[1] that the copper issues of the Urtuḳís, etc., were intended to pass as *dirhams*. There is much in favour of this view, besides the occurrence of the word *dirham* on some of the coins. There can be no doubt that *dirham* at that time meant the same thing as on the coins of the 'Abbásí Khalífahs, namely, a *silver* coin, and that it was not used in a general way (like the plurals of *fals* and *dirham* in modern Arabic) to mean any kind of money. Nor can we suppose that the word was introduced by mistake, instead of فلس *fals*; for it occurs on too many coins to be explained by any hypothetical carelessness of the engravers. Granting, then, that when the Urtuḳís put the name *dirham* on their coins they meant *dirham* and not *fals*, and rejecting the suggestion that the name was inserted by mistake, it is difficult to see how to arrive at any conclusion except that these coins were intended to pass for the same value as silver dirhams. And it would be absurd to limit this to the coins that bear the word *dirham*, for the other copper coins are precisely similar in size and general aspect, with the exception of the curse-formula. We must, therefore, in all reason extend the denomination *dirham* beyond those coins on which the word is found to the whole class of large copper of the same series. A circumstance much in favour of the theory is that many of the large copper coins are covered with a thin coating of silver,[2] and those that are thus ornamented do not bear the name *dirham*. Of course a difficulty arises from the fact that only some, and not all, these coins are silvered. Yet this may perhaps be explained by supposing them to have been silvered with a view to giving a look of respectability to the rest. The entire absence of *silver dirhams* during the period of the issuing of the large copper coins by the Urtuḳís is greatly in favour of Dr. Karabacek's theory; but it is almost counterbalanced by the fact that after the introduction of a silver coinage by Urtuḳ-Arslán of Máridín, the copper coinage still continued, though certainly in less numbers and perhaps smaller size. It is difficult to believe that silver and copper dirhams should circulate together, issuing from the same mint; or, on the other hand, that copper coins which had recently possessed the value of silver dirhams should suddenly, on the introduction of silver dirhams, be degraded to the value of ordinary *fulús*. This, in fact, taken together with the small number of silvered dirhams that have been preserved, forms the main obstacle to Dr. Karabacek's view of the denomination of the Urtuḳí coinage. With regard to the origin of the copper image-coinage, Dr. Karabacek thinks it may be traced to the copper issues of the Latin princes whom the Crusading mania had brought to Syria; and that the principal reason of the substitution of copper for silver was the general exhaustion which oppressed the countries afflicted by the so-called 'Holy War,' and which rendered a silver coinage impossible.

Whilst acknowledging the strength of the arguments in favour of the dirham-view of the

on the Urtuḳí coins. 'عَيَّرَ الدَّنَا نِيرٌ *he weighed the pieces of gold one after another*; and, *he put*, or *threw down, the pieces of gold, one by one, and compared them, one by one*.' In other words, this form of the verb means, in this application, to *test* or *check* or *prove* money, in order to see whether it is good. The connexion of this meaning with the primary meaning of عَيَّر, to upbraid or *declare a thing to be bad*, is easily seen; for testing a coin implies the suspicion that it is bad. There is, after all, not much difference between this and Dr. Karabacek's rendering of the word.

[1] Bd. i. (1869) pp. 265-300.
[2] In the British Museum there is one Urtuḳí coin which is *gilded* instead of *silvered*.

Urtuḳí coinage, it is to be regretted that we have not more positive evidence on the subject. At present, though the weight of the evidence leans heavily to Dr. Karabacek's side, it must be admitted that his point is not yet absolutely proved.

§ 6. The copper coins, which form the great majority of the Urtuḳí mintage, range in weight from 2·8 to 17·0 grammes (43 to 263 English grains); and in diameter from IV to XI on Mionnet's scale ($\frac{7}{10}$ to $1\frac{1}{4}$ English inch). The average weight may be placed at about 11 grammes (170 grains), and the average diameter at about VIII ($1\frac{1}{8}$ inch) of Mionnet's scale.

The few silver coins of the series weigh about 2·9 grammes, and are of the diameter of Mionnet's V. The weight, it will be observed, nearly corresponds with that of the old Amawí and 'Abbásí dirham.

TABLE I.—SUZERAINS TO WHOM THE URTUḲÍS DID HOMAGE ON THEIR COINS.

	SUZERAIN.		VASSAL.
Ayyúbís	Ṣaláḥ-ad-dín	M.[1]	Yúluḳ-Arslán, 581, 583, 584, 585, 586.
		K.	Sukmán II., 581, 584.
	Al-'Ádil........................	M.	Yúluḳ-Arslán, 589.
			Urtuḳ-Arslán, 599, 606, 611.
		K.	Maḥmúd, 615.
	Al-Kámil	M.	Urtuḳ-Arslán, 615, 620, 628, 630.
		K.	Maḥmúd, 610?, 617, 618.
	Aẓ-Ẓáhir	M.	Urtuḳ-Arslán, 599.
	Al-'Azíz (of Ḥalab).........	M.	Urtuḳ-Arslán.
	An-Náṣir Ṣaláḥ-ad-dín II...	M.	Najm-ad-dín Ghází, 654, 655, 656, 657, [658.
	As-Ṣáliḥ Ayyúb	M.	Najm-ad-dín Ghází, 645, 646.
	Al-Afḍal and Aẓ-Ẓáhir ...	M.	Yúluḳ-Arslán, 596.
	Al-Kámil and Al-Ashraf...	K.	Maudúd, 621.
Atábég of Al-Mauṣil ..	Núr-ad-dín Arslán Sháh[2]..	M.	Yúluḳ-Arslán, 596.
Saljúḳis of Ar-Rúm ...	Kay-Káwus	K.	Maḥmúd, 614.
	Kay-Ḳubád.................	M.	Urtuḳ-Arslán, 623, 625, 634.
	Kay-Khusrú II.	M.	Urtuḳ-Arslán, 634.
			Najm-ad-dín Ghází, 640–3.
Moguls of Persia	Húlágú	M.	Ḳará-Arslán.

[1] M. represents Máridín; K. Kayfá. The figures after the name of the Urtuḳí vassal show the years in which he acknowledged the suzerainty of his liege-lord on his own coins. I have not included the 'Abbásí Khalífahs among the suzerains of the Urtuḳís, although their names often appear on the coinage of these princes; they merely exercised a spiritual suzerainty, and barely that.

[2] This name appears on the same coin as the names of Al-Afḍal and Aẓ-Ẓáhir, mentioned above.

Table II.—Dynasties Contemporary with the Urtuḳí Turkumáns.

A.D.	A.H.	Urtuḳís of Kayfá.	Urtuḳís of Máridín.	Urtuḳís of Ḥalab.	Atábegs of Al-Mauṣil.	Atábegs of Ḥalab.	Atábegs of Sinjár.	Saljúḳís of Persia.	Saljúḳís of Ar-Rúm.	Saljúḳís of Damascus.	Ayyúbis.	'Abbásí Khalífahs.	Kings of Jerusalem.	Emperors of Constantinople.	A.H.	A.D.
1072	465							Malik-Sháh.							465	1072
1078	471									Tutush.					471	1078
1081	474													Alexius I. Comnenus.	474	1081
1086	479								Ḳilij-Arslán I.						479	1086
1092	485							Barjiyáruḳ.							485	1092
1094	487									Daḳḳáḳ.		Al-Mustaẓhir.			487	1094
1098	492												Godfrey of Bouillon.		492	1098
1099	493												Baldwin I.		493	1099
1101	495	Sukmán.								Búrís.					495	1101
1103	497									Tughtakin.					497	1103
1104	498	Ibráhím.						Muḥammad.							498	1104
1106	500								Mas'úd I.						500	1106
1108	502	Dáwúd.	Íl-Ghází.												502	1108
1114	508				Aḳsunḳur.										508	1114
1117	511			Sulaymán ibn Íl-Ghází.				Sinjar, d. 552					Baldwin II.		511	1117
								Saljúḳís of 'Al-Iráḳ.								
1118	512							Maḥmúd.				Al-Mustarshid		John II.	512	1118
1121	515			Sulaymán ibn 'Abd-al-Jabbár.											515	1121
1122	516		Timurtásh.												516	1122
1123	517			Balak.											517	1123
1126	520				Mas'úd I.										520	1126
1127	521				Zangí I.										521	1127
1128	522									Táj-al-Mulúk Búrí.					522	1128
1130	525							Ṭughril.					Fulk of Anjou		525	1130
1131	526									Isma'íl.					526	1131
1133	528								Mas'úd II.						528	1133
1134	529							Mas'úd.		Maḥmúd.		Ar-Ráshid.			529	1134
1135	530											Al-Muktafí.			530	1135
1138	533									Muḥammad.					533	1138
1139	534									Abaḳ.					534	1139
1141	536												Baldwin III.		536	1141
1142	537												Amaury.	Manuel I.	537	1142
1146	541				Ghází I.	Núr-ad-dín Maḥmúd. (*Noureddin*).									541	1146
1148	543	Kará-Arslán.													543	1148
1149	544				Maudúd I.										544	1149
1152	547		Alpi.					Malik-Sháh. Muḥammad.		Dominions taken by Núr-ad-dín of Ḥalab.					547	1152
1156	551								Ḳilij-Arslán II.						551	1156
1159	554							Sulaymán. Arslán.							554	1159

1169	565				Ghází II.		Zangi.							565	1169
1170	566										Al-Mustaḍí.			566	1170
1171	567									Ṣaláḥ-ad-dín (*Saladin*). [Sons:— Al-Afḍal. Al-'Azíz. Az-Ẓáhir.				567	1171
1172	568											Baldwin IV.		568	1172
1173	569					Isma'íl.								569	1173
1174	570	Muḥammad.												570	1174
1175	571							Ṭugbril. d. 590.						571	1175
1176	572		Il-Ghází II.											572	1176
1179	575										An-Náṣir.		Alexius II.	575	1179
1180	576				Mas'úd II.									576	1180
1181	577					Ṣaláḥ-ad-dín takes Ḥalab.								577	1181
1182	578			URTUKÍS OF KHARTAPIRT.								Baldwin V.	Andronicus I.	578	1182
1184	580		Yúluḳ-Arslán										Isaac II.	580	1184
1185	581	Sukmán II.		Abú-Bakr.								Guy of Lusignan.		581	1185
1187	583											Jerusalem taken by Ṣaláḥ-ad-dín		583	1187
1192	588								Sulaymán II.					588	1192
1193	589				Arslán-Sháh.					Al-'Ádil.				589	1193
1194	591												Alexius III.	591	1194
1197	594						Muḥammad.							594	1197
1200	597	Maḥmúd.	Urtuḳ-Arslán.											597	1200
1202	599												Isaac *rest.*	599	1202
1203	600			Abú-Bakr II. d. 620.					Kay-Khusrú I.					600	1203
1206	603												Henry.	603	1206
1210	607				Mas'úd III.				Kay-Káwus.					607	1210
1216	613												Peter.	613	1216
1218	615				Arslán-Sháh II.					Al-Kámil.				615	1218
1219	616				Maḥmúd.		Sháhán-Sháh. Maḥmúd or 'Umar.		Kay-Ḳubád I.					616	1219
1220	617						Surrender to Ayyúbís.							617	1220
1222	619	Maudúd.			Lu-lu.									619	1222
1225	622										Aẓ-Ẓáhir.			622	1225
1226	623										Al-Mustanṣir			623	1226
1228	626												John of Brienne	626	1228
1231	629	Subversion of Dynasty by Ayyúbís.												629	1231
1236	634								Kay-Khusrú II.					634	1236
1237	635												Baldwin II.	635	1237
1239	637		Ghází.											637	1239
1242	640										Al-Musta'ṣim d. 656.			640	1242
			etc.						etc.	etc.			etc.		

TABLE III.—CHRONOLOGICAL LIST OF THE URTUḲÍ PRINCES.

I. KAYFÁ LINE. A.H. 495–629.

i. Sukmán I. 495.
ii. Ibráhím. 498.
iii. Dáwúd. *c.* 502.
iv. Ḳará-Arslán. *c.* 543.
v. Muḥammad. 570.
vi. Sukmán II. 581.
vii. Maḥmúd. 597.
viii. Maudúd. 619–629.

II. KHARTAPIRT LINE. A.H. 581–620.

i. Abú-Bakr I. 581.
ii. Abú-Bakr II. *c.* 600–620.

III. MÁRIDÍN LINE. A.H. 502–715, etc.

i. Íl-Ghází I. 502.
ii. Timurtásh. 516.
iii. Alpí. 547.
iv. Íl-Ghází II. 572.
v. Yúluḳ-Arslán. 580.
vi. Urtuḳ-Arslán. *c.* 597.
vii. Ghází. 637.
viii. Ḳará-Arslán. 658.
ix. Dáwúd. *c.* 691.
x. Ghází II. *c.* 693.
xi. 'Alí Alpí. 712.
xii. Ṣáliḥ. 712–715, etc.[1]

[1] Shams-ad-dín Ṣáliḥ was still reigning when Abu-l-Fida wrote his history in A.H. 715.

TABLE IV.—GENEALOGICAL TREE OF THE HOUSE OF URTUḲ.

- URTUḲ [*Jerusalem*, 479–484.]
  - Sukmán *Mu'ín-ad-daulah* [*Jerusalem*, 484–489: *Sarúj*, 488: *Ḥiṣn Kayfá*, 495: *Máridín*, *c.* 496.
    - Ibráhím [*Kayfá & Máridín*, 498.
    - Dáwúd *Rukn-ad-daulah* [*Kayfá*, *c.* 502?
      - Ḳará-Arslán *Fakhr-ad-dín* [*Kayfá*, *c.* 543.
        - Muḥammad *Núr-ad-dín* [*Kayfá*, 570: *Ámid*, 579.
          - Sukmán II. *Kuṭb-ad-dín* [*Kayfá & Ámid*, 581.
          - Maḥmúd *Náṣir-ad-dín* [*Kayfá & Ámid*, 597.
            - Maudúd *Rukn-ad-dín* [*Kayfá & Ámid*, 619–629.
        - Abú-bakr *'Imád-ad-dín* [*Khartapirt*, 581.
          - Abú-bakr *Niẓám-ad-dín* [*Khartapirt*, *c.* 600 to 620.
  - 'Abd-Al-Jabbár
    - Sulaymán *Badr-ad-daulah*, [*Ḥalab*, 515–517.
  - Íl-Ghází *Najm-ad-dín* [*Shaḥnah of Baghdád* 495–502: *Máridín*, 502: *Ḥalab*, 511: *Mayyáfáriḳín*, 515.
    - Timurtásh *Ḥusám-ad-dín* [*Máridín*, 516: *Ḥalab*, 518, for a short time: *Mayyáfáriḳín*, 518.
      - Alpí *Najm-ad-dín* [*Máridín*, etc., 547.
        - Íl-Ghází II. *Kuṭb-ad-dín* [*Máridín*, etc., 572.
          - Yúluḳ-Arslán *Ḥusám-ad-dín* [*Máridín*, 580.
          - Urtuḳ-Arslán *Náṣir-ad-dín* [*Máridín*, *c.* 597.
            - Ghází *Najm-ad-dín* [*Máridín*, 637.
              - Ḳárá-Arslán [*Máridín*, 658.
    - Ayáz
    - Sulaymán *Shams-ad-daulah* [*Mayyáfáriḳín*, 516 died 518.
  - Bahrám
    - Balak [*Sarúj* (in Sukmán's name?) 488?–494: *'Ánah*, etc., 497: *Ḥarrán*, 517: *Ḥalab*, 517: died 518.
    - Yáḳúti [*Máridín* circ. 496.
    - 'Alí [*Máridín* circ. 496.
    - Maḥmúd *Shiháb-ad-dín* [*Al-Bírah* before 565.
      - Son [*Al-Bírah* before 577.

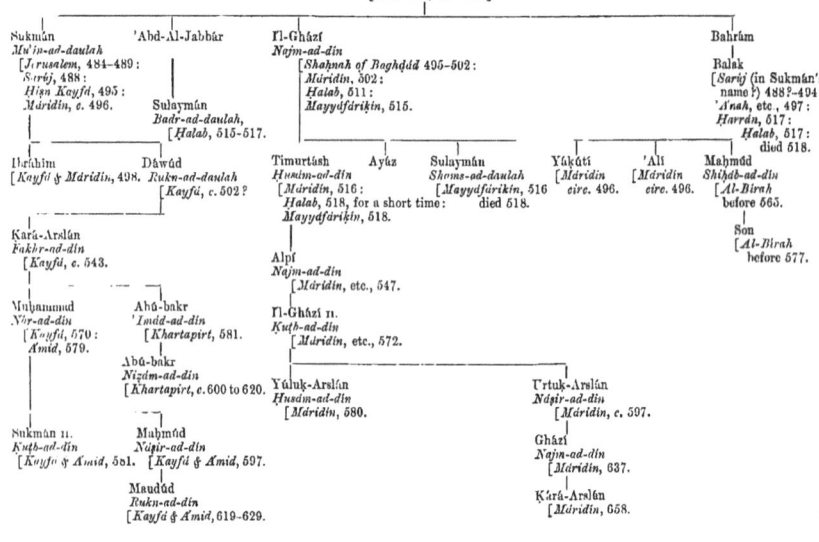

COINS OF THE URTUḲI'S.

I. URTUḲI'S OF KAYFA.

IV. Fakhr-ad-dín Ḳará-arslán. A.H. *circ.* 543–570.

Type I.

1. Copper. (Pl. i. fig. cxlvii.) A.H. 556. (British Museum. *Num. Chron.* vol. xiii. p. 284, no. 1.)

Obv. Half-figure to right: in left hand, sceptre; in right, orb.
[Copied, probably, from a common late-Byzantine type, seen on the coins of Constantine vi. and Eirene.]
(Margin: سنة ثنو)

Rev.
بن داود
الملك العا
لم العادل
فخر الدين
(Margins: قرارسلان — بن ارتق)
Below, fleuron.

No points except the diacritical points of ثنو and the ن of سنة. ثنو represents 556;[1] the numerical value of ث being 500, of ن 50, and of و 6. The ا of قرا is omitted, as on many other examples.

Type II.

2. Copper. (Pl. iv. fig. 1.) A.H. 559. (The late Col. C. S. Guthrie's Collection.)[2]

Obv. Half-figure, facing, crowned.
(Margins: في سنة تسع — و خمسين و خمس مائة)

Rev. A. Half-figure, facing, bare-headed.
M. الملك العادل فخر الدين قرارسلان بن داود
بن ارتق

The first stroke of the س of سنة is taller than the others; the ى of في and the ن of سنة are dotted; so, too, the خ and ى of خمس مائة (خمس مايه).

Type III.

3. Copper. (Pl. iv. fig. 2.) A.H. 560. (British Museum. *Num. Chron.* no. 3.)

Obv.
لا اله الا الله
Head, facing.
(Margins: المستنجد بالله — محمد رسول الله)

Rev.
ملك الامرا
قرا ارسلان بن
داود بن سكمان
بن ارتق
(Margins: سنة ستين — وخمسمائة)

Diacritical points on reverse to ن of سنة, خ and ى of خمسمائة, ق of قرا, ن of أرسلان and of بن and of سكمان, and a line (representing the two points) over ت of ستّين. The ق of أرتق is prolonged into a foliate ornament.

[1] It is remarkable that this simple explanation has never before been proposed, except by myself in the *Num. Chron.* vol. xiii. p. 284.

[2] In the British Museum there is another specimen similar to this, but rather inferior in condition, which has been described by me in the *Num. Chron.* vol. xiii. p. 380.

Type IV.

1.

4. Copper. (Pl. iv. fig. 3.) A.H. 562. (British Museum. *Num. Chron.* no. 5.)

Obv.				Rev.			
	وستين و خمسمائة	Half-figure, facing. [Copied, perhaps, from a Byzantine coin representing the Virgin.]	سنة اثنين		المستنجد بالله	ملــك الامرا قرا ارسلان بــن داود بـــــن سكمان بن ارتق	الامام

The ن of سنة, the خ and ى of خمسمائة, the ت and ن of المستنجد, have their proper diacritical points; though in the case of the ى of مائة the diacritical points can scarcely be called proper, as the letter serves for the base of hemz and therefore should not be dotted.

A variety in the British Museum differs only in points, and not much in them, so far as the indistinctness of the coin permits me to judge.

2.

5. Copper. (Pl. iv. fig. 4.) A.H. 570. (British Museum. *Num. Chron.* no. 7.)

Same: but small winged figure, to left, behind left shoulder of central figure; and, on the opposite side of figure, date سبعين و خمسمائة.

Diacritical points to the ت and ن of المستنجد.

3.

6. Copper. A.H. 570. (Faba Collection, 450.)[1]

Same as preceding, but rev. marg. الامام | المستضى بامر الله instead of الامام | المستنجد بالله and rev. area داوود instead of داود.

Until I was informed of the existence of this last coin I was inclined to think that Ibn-al-Athír was correct in his date of Ḳará-Arslán's death (A.H. 562), and that the occurrence of that prince's name on a coin of the year 570 (no. 5) was to be explained by Núr-ad-dín having omitted to alter the reverse of his father's coin when he changed the date. But no. 6, besides confirming the date 570, brings further evidence by the name of the Khalífah Al-Mustaḍí, who did not begin to reign till 565, three years after the death of Ḳará-Arslán, as recorded by Ibn-al-Athír. We cannot choose but to accept the testimony of these two monuments, and to place the death of Ḳará-Arslán at 570, or the earlier part of 571. No coin of Núr-ad-dín is known of an earlier date than 571, and this too goes to support the evidence of the two coins of Ḳará-Arslán. One difficulty remains—the coincidence of the name of the Khalífah Al-Mustanjid, who died in 565, on the coin bearing the date 570. This I think must be explained by the suggestion I offered before as to the reverse of Ḳará-Arslán's fourth type having been left unchanged when the date on the obverse was altered: the difference I now make in the explanation is that it was left unchanged by Ḳará-Arslán himself, whereas before I supposed that it was his son Núr-ad-dín who had altered the date, but not the reverse.

The orthography داوود is very unusual. Ordinarily the name is written داود, in which case the و should be marked with *maddah* (داوٓد) to show that it is a contraction for وُو. The transliteration Dá-úd (based upon the vulgar pronunciation دَاوُود) is incorrect; it should be Dáwúd.

[1] Brought to my notice by Dr. Blau, Kaiserlich deutscher, General-Consul, Odessa.

Type V.

7. Copper. (Pl. iv. fig. 5.) (British Museum. *Num. Chron.* no. 9.)

OBV. A. Full figure of winged Victory to right; holding in right hand tablet inscribed VOT / XXX, and in left hand wreath; beneath SIS.

M. VICTORIACONSTANTINIAUG.

[Copied from a coin of Constantine, struck at Siscia, in Pannonia.]

REV.

بن داود
الملك العا
لم العادل
فخرالدين

(margins) ارتق بن — قرا ارسلان

Beneath, ornament.

Type VI.

1.

8. Copper. (British Museum. *Num. Chron.* no. 11.)

OBV. اجد — طه / حرو

(margins) المومنين — امير / معين

The common late-Byzantine type of Christ, aureolate, sitting on throne, holding book.

[The type may be seen on coins of Manuel I. Comnenus.]

REV.

بن داود
الملك العا
لم العادل
فخرالدين

(margins) ارتق بن — قرا ارسلان

On the obv. diacritical points under the three ىs;[1] and over the first ن of المومنين.

On the rev. semicircles over the ع s of العالم and العادل, muhmilahs over the م of لم and the خ of فخر, and shaddah over the د of الدين. The ب and ن of both بنs are dotted, also the خ of فخر and the ى of الدين.

2.

9. Copper. (British Museum. *Num. Chron.* no. 13.)

٦٣٥ ٤٩٢ is substituted for اجد طه / حرو

Points, etc., as (8).

3.

10. Copper. (Pl. iv. fig. 6.) (British Museum. *Num. Chron.* no. 14.)

Same as (9), but a countermark, of unintelligible device, is struck on the obv. left, near the bottom.

No muhmilahs, etc.

The letters and ciphers on the obverse of these coins have never been interpreted, and I do not think any meaning can be attached to them. The explanation of their occurrence which I venture to offer is that the Oriental engraver, unable to decipher the Greek inscriptions IC, XC, of the original Byzantine coin, substituted whatever Arabic letters or ciphers first came into his head. The analogy of other coins of the series does not permit us to assume that religious scruples were the cause of the change. It is worth noting that the ciphers which occur on (9) comprise the ten digits, neither more nor less: ٠١٢٣٤٥٦٧٨٩.[2]

[1] The two dots under معين are blundered, so as to form a short horizontal line.

[2] It has been suggested that the *letters* on (8) are arranged regularly in the order of the older *abjad* ابجد هوز حطى, etc. There is certainly something to justify this view. The four letters on the left-hand-side might very well be ابجد, though it is hard to see why the ج and د are not connected. Beyond the first four letters, however, the order of the abjad is not easily discovered. We should have to change حرو into هوز and طه into حطى.

Type VII.

11. Copper. (Pl. iv. fig. 7.) (Col. Guthrie's Collection.)

Obv. Bust of Christ, head surrounded by an aureole of six rays; two dots between alternate pairs of rays. In the field, IC XC and a cross ✛, and signs designed apparently to represent the letters EMMANOTHA.

[A common Byzantine type.]

Rev.

بن ارتق
ضرب هذا
الدرهم ايام
فخر الدين
قرا ارسلان

(margins) بن سكمان — بن داود

A specimen (*a*) in the British Museum (*Num. Chron.* no. 16) differs from that described above only in having a line over XC as well as over IC. Another specimen (*b*) differs from (11) in having four dots instead of two between the alternate rays of the aureole, and فى inserted between الدرهم and ايام (*ibid.* no. 15).

The expression "in the days of Ḳará-Arslán" seems to point to the coin not having been struck by Ḳará-Arslán himself, but by some governor under him.

V. Núr-ad-dín Muḥammad. A.H. 570–581.

Type I.

12. Copper. (Pl. i. fig. CLIII.) A.H. 571. (British Museum. *Num. Chron.* no. 17.)

Obv. Angel, aureolate; right wing raised; left hand holding scroll, which hangs over right arm.

(margins) وخمسمائة — سنة احد وسبعين

Rev.

ملك الامرا محمد
بن قرا ارسلان بن
داود بن سكما
ن بن ارتق نصير
امير المومنين

(margins) المستضي بامر الله — الامام

In the Guthrie collection there is a specimen (*a*) differing from (12) only in omitting the ا of قرا.

Type II.

13. Copper. (Pl. i. fig. CLV.) A.H. 576. (British Museum. *Num. Chron.* no. 19.)

Obv. Within cusped pointed arch of double lines, figure, seated on throne; in right hand orb, in left sceptre. Two balls represent the arms of the throne. Above the arch two angels, each spreading a wing over the acme of the arch.

(margins) سنة ست وسبعين — وخمس مائة

Rev. Within square,

ملك الامرا محمد
بن قرا ارسلان بن
داود بن سكمان
بن ارتق نصيرا

Around: الناصر — لدين الله — مير المو — منين الامام

On this coin the final letters of محمد and داود and the ك of سكمان and the ص of نصير terminate in an ornament; which, however, Marsden's engraver has omitted to represent in the plate.

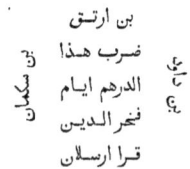

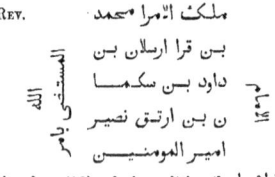

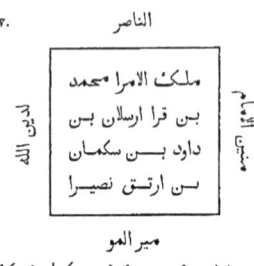

Type III.

14. Copper. (Pl. iv. fig. 8.) Al-Ḥiṣn. [Kayfá.] A.H. 578. (British Museum. *Num. Chron.* no. 21.)

OBV. A. Head to left, diademed.

[Copied from coin of Seleukus II., but reversed; the engraver having copied the coin directly on to the die, without first reversing it.]

M. على اسم الله ضرب بالحصن سنة ثمان
وسبعين وخمس مائة

REV. ملك الامرا محيى
العدل نور الدين
محمد بن قرا ارسلا
ن بن ارتق نصير
الامام الناصر
لدين الله

At sides: ملعون من يعيره

The expression عَلَى ٱسْمِ ٱللّٰه *'ala-smi-llâh* for بِسْمِ ٱللّٰه *bi-smi-llâh* is most uncommon. The curse مَلْعُون مَن يُعَيِّره, which so long puzzled numismatists, is translated (in its full form as it occurs on coins of Il-Ghází II. of Máridín—no. 35 ff.) by Dr. Karabacek (*Num. Zeit.* Wien, 1869) *Verflucht sei, wer diesem Dirhem einen Schimpf anthut, Cursed be he who puts an affront upon this dirhem*, i.e. *dishonours it*, or *damages its credit*. It may better perhaps be rendered *Cursed be he who tests this dirhem* (see p. 9, note 4). مُحَيِّي ٱلْعَدْل *The reviver of equity* has been differently read, but there can be no question that this, which was published by Castiglioni, is the true form; and that the other suggestions, such as عين العدل, were founded on ill-preserved specimens.

VI. Ḳuṭb-ad-dín Sukmán II. A.H. 581–597.

Type I.

1.

15. Copper. Al-Ḥiṣn. [Kayfá.] A.H. 581. (British Museum. *Num. Chron.* no. 23.)

OBV. A. Bearded head of king to left.

[Copied from Sassanian coins.]

M. على اسم الله ضرب بالحصن سنة احد
وثمانين وخمس مائة

(The last two words (خمس مائة) are in an inner line, for want of space in the outer.)

REV. لدين الله

In square:
الملك العادل قطب
الدين سكمان بن
محمد بن قرا ارسلان
بن ارتق معين الاما

م الناصر

At sides: ملعون من يعيره

Ornament attached to the ك of سكمان.

2.

16. Copper. (Pl. iv. fig. 9.) Al-Ḥiṣn. [Kayfá.] A.H. 581. (Guthrie Collection.)[1]

At sides of rev. الملك الناصر | صلاح الدين instead of ملعون من | يعيره, and the و preceding خمس مائة in obv. marg. is in the inner line with خمس مائة.

This is the first occurrence of the name of a liege-lord (except the spiritual suzerain, the Khalífah) on Urtuḳí coins. In the same year Ṣaláḥ-ad-dín's name occurs also for the first time on the coins of Yúluḳ-Arslán of Máridín (cp. no. 42).

[1] A similar coin belonging to the British Museum is published in the *Num. Chron.* xiii. 293, no. 24.

Type II.

17. Copper. (Pl. v. fig. 1.)[1] A.H. 584. (British Museum. *Num. Chron.* no. 25.)

OBV. سنة اربع وثمنين و
خمسمئة

Two heads, back to back.

[Copied from coin of Augustus and Agrippa struck at Nemausus (Nismes).]

REV. لدين الله
الملك العادل قطب
الدين سكمان بن
محمد بن قرا ارسلان
بن ارتق معين الاما
م الناصر

(Left margin) يوسف بن ايوب
(Right margin) الملك الناصر

Another specimen (*a*) in the British Museum (*Num. Chron.* no. 26) differs only in having the م in the same line as الاما; and the و in the same line as خمسمئة.

Type III.

18. Copper. (Pl. v. fig. 2.)[2] A.H. 594. (British Museum. *Num. Chron.* no. 28.)

OBV. A. Half figure facing, with helmet, and aureole; holding in right hand sceptre; in left, orb.

[The idea seems to have been taken from a Byzantine type of about the time of Justinian I.; but the aureole is unaccountable.]

M. سنة اربع وتسعين وخمس مائة

REV. الامام
الملك المسعود
قطب الدين سكمان
بن محمد بن قرا
ارسلان

(Left margin) الناصر امير
(Right margin) المؤمنين

Over the first letter of سكمان, ornament like the sign for Aries, between two points.

In the Guthrie collection there is a specimen (*a*) similar to (18), but the points in the field of the reverse are wanting, although the ornament remains.

VII. NÁṢIR-AD-DÍN MAḤMÚD. A.H. 597–619.

Type I.

1.

19. Copper. (Pl. v. fig. 3.) Ámid. A.H. 614. (British Museum. *Num. Chron.* no. 31.)

OBV. A. Two-headed Imperial Eagle (*each wing formed by a man's bearded head*) standing on pedestal of interwoven lines.

(Left margin) سنة ٦١٤
(Right margin) ضرب بآمد

M. الملك الصالح ناصر الدنيا والدين ا
محمود بن محمد بن ارتق ♈

REV. الامام الناصر
السلطان الغالب
عز الدنيا والدين
كيكاوس بن كيخسرو
بن قلج ارسلان
* ♈ *

(Left margin) امير
(Right margin) المؤمنين

Another example (*a*) in the British Museum has a muhmilah over the س of كيخسرو. A third example

[1] An imperfect specimen belonging to the Marsden Collection is engraved in Pl. i. fig. CLIV.

[2] An imperfect specimen belonging to the Marsden Collection is engraved in Pl. i. fig. CLIX.

(*b*) differs from (19) in that الدين is divided, ين being put in the lower line; and لب of الغالب is treated in like fashion.

This is the only occasion on which the name of the Saljúḳí Sulṭán of Anatolia (or Rúm) appears on the coins of the Kayfá and A'mid family.

20. Copper. Al-Ḥiṣn. [Kayfá.] A.H. 615. (British Museum. *Num. Chron.* no. 34.)

OBV. Imperial eagle as before, but wings not human; pedestal different from preceding; and ☾ on eagle's breast.

(Margins: سنة ٦١٥ — ضرب بالحصن)

REV.
الامام
الملك الصالح
محمود بن ارتق
الملك العادل
ابوبكر

(Margins: الناصر امير — المومنين)

٧ over م of the first الملك, ص and ح of الصالح, و of محمود, and م of the second الملك. Point over ن of المومنين and of بن.

Another specimen (*a*) in the British Museum (Pl. v. fig. 4) differs in having no muhmilahs over the two الملكs, and no point over بن.

Al-Malik Al-'A'dil Abú-Bakr, whose name appears on this coin as that of liege-lord, was the brother of Ṣaláḥ-ad-dín. He died this same year 615.

21. Copper. (Pl. i. fig. CLVIII.) A'mid. A.H. 617. (British Museum. *Num. Chron.* no. 36.)

OBV. A. Imperial eagle as before, but smaller, and inclosed in a circular figure formed by the intersection of two quasi-ovals, which are surrounded by a plain circle and an outer dotted circle.

M. Inner. الملك | الصالح | ناصر | الدين

Outer. محمود | بن محمد | بن قرارسلان | بن ارتق

REV. Hexagram, within circle.

In centre, الملك
الكامل

In the triangular spaces between lines of hexagram,
ضرب | بامد | سنة | سبع | عشر | ستمائة

In spaces between hexagram and circle,
الامام | الناصر | احمد | ناصر | الدين | محمد

Point over ن of بن محمد on obverse. Three points over the ش of عشر on reverse.

A variety (*a*) in the British Museum has the obverse margin divided محمود بن | محمد, instead of محمود | بن محمد (*Num. Chron.* no. 37).

Al-Malik Al-Kámil Náṣir-ad-dín Muḥammad was son and principal successor of Al-'A'dil.

22. Copper. (Pl. v. fig. 5.) A.H. 610? (British Museum. *Num. Chron.* no. 39.)

OBV. A. Imperial eagle within circle.

M. ناصر الدنيا والدين محمود . . ؟

REV.
عشر ؟
الامام الناصر
لدين الله امير
المومنين الملك
الكامل محمد بن ؟
ابوبكر

(Margins: ستمائة — ضرب . . . .)

The two-headed eagle was apparently the armorial badge of the city of A'mid. The first coin struck at that city since the introduction of images on Muḥammadan coins bears this eagle; and Ramusio[1] records that he observed it on many parts of the walls of Ámid. He does not seem, however, to have remarked any eagles with grotesque wings formed of the bearded heads of men, such as appear on the coin described above (19).

The origin of the two-headed eagle is very obscure. One thing alone is certain, that it was known in the East long before it was adopted by the Emperors of Germany. We find it on coins of 'Imád-ad-dín Zangí of Sinjár, struck in the year 1190 (A.H. 586), and on Urtuḳí coins of 1217 (614); whilst the Emperors did not make use of it till the year 1345.[2] M. de Longpérier[3] believes that he has discovered the clue to the history of this eagle in a relief at the village of Boghar Kieui, in Asia Minor, on which are represented two attendants of one of the principal ancient divinities, placed upright on a two-headed eagle. Further, on the side of a block of stone (the front of which is hewn into the form of a giant bird), at Euyuk, is cut the figure of a two-headed eagle, which M. de Longpérier conjectures to have been sculptured by the Saljúḳís in imitation of the ancient relief at Boghar Kieui, which may very probably have struck them by its resemblance to the fabulous bird the 'Anḳá, described as the greatest of birds, carrying off elephants as a kite carries off a mouse.[4] The Urtuḳís and Atábégs then copied the eagle from the Saljúḳís; and, finally, the Flemish Counts, in their intercourse with the Saljúḳís, became acquainted with the device and introduced it to Europe.

Type II.

23. Copper. (Pl. v. fig. 6.) A.H. 618? (British Museum. *Num. Chron.* no. 40.)

OBV. Man on lion, holding in right hand short sword; behind, Urtuḳí damghah.

محمود [illegible]

ناصر

REV. A.

الملك الصالح
الملك الكامل
محمد

M. الامام | الناصر | اميرالمو | منين | ضرب |
سنة | ثمان عشر؟

VIII. RUKN-AD-DÍN MAUDÚD. A.H. 619–629.

Type I.

24. Copper. Ámid. A.H. 621. (British Museum. *Num. Chron.* no. 43.)

OBV. Small Imperial eagle, in circle, within square, within second circle, the whole surrounded by dotted circle.

In spaces between inner circle and square.

ضرب | بامد | سنة | ٦٢١

In spaces between square and outer circle,

الملك المسعود | ركن الدين | مودود بن |
محمود بن ارتق

REV. Same arrangement of circles and square as on obv., except that the centre circle is ornamented with four loops.

Within inner circle, الملك الكامل

In spaces between inner circle and square,

الملك | الا | شرف | موسى

In spaces between square and outer circle,

لا اله الا الله | محمد رسول [الله] | الامام الناصر |
لدين الله امير المومنين

Another specimen (*a*) in the British Museum (*Num. Chron.* no. 44) has the date reversed ١٦٢. (Pl. v. fig. 7.) The use of ciphers instead of the regular numerals is very unusual on these coins.

[1] *Delle Navicazioni e viaggi raccolti da Gio. Batt.* RAMUSIO, ii. 79 (Venet. 1606).
[2] GATTERER, *Comm. Soc. Götting.* x. 241.
[3] LONGPÉRIER (Review of Texier and Hamilton), *Rev. Archéol.* ii. (old series).
[4] LANE, *Thousand and One Nights*, xx. note 22. In the Guthrie Collection is a remarkable coin representing the Rókh or 'Anḳá carrying off several elephants in its talons.

II. URTUḲI'S OF KHARTAPIRT.

I. 'Imád-ad-dín Abú-Bakr. A.H. 581–*circ.* 600.

Type I.

25. Copper. (Pl. v. fig. 8.) A.H. 585. (Guthrie Collection.)

Obv. Figure, almost naked, on serpent; tail of serpent coiled six times; extremity held in left hand of figure.

Rev.

الملك الامرا محيى
العدل عماد الدين
ابو بكر بن قرا ارسلا
ن بن ارتق نصير
الامام الناصر
لدين الله

(left margin) خمس وثمانين
(right margin) وخمسمائة

The British Museum possesses an example of this excessively rare coin,[1] but its condition is not quite equal to that of the specimen contained in the Guthrie Collection.

Type II.

26. Copper. (Pl. v. fig. 9.) A.H. 588. (Guthrie Collection.)

Obv. Head to left, diademed.

Rev.

ملك الامرا
ابو بكر بن
قرا ارسلان
بن ارتق النا
صر لدين الله
[illegible]

(left margin) ثمان ثمانين
(right margin) سنة

There are two specimens of this type (*Num. Chron.* nos. 47, 48) in the British Museum, but neither of them is quite equal in preservation to that of the Guthrie Collection.

[1] It is described in the *Num. Chron.* xiii. p. 301, no. 46; but the illustration of the obverse in the plate accompanying the article was photographed from a cast of Col. Guthrie's specimen, of which both sides are now exhibited in Pl. v. fig. 8.

III. URTUKÍS OF MÁRIDÍN.

II. Ḥusám-ad-dín Timurtásh. A.H. 516–547.

Type I.

27. Copper. (British Museum. *Num. Chron.* no. 49.)

Obv. Head to right. [Copied from coin of Antiochus vii.]	Rev. ایل غازی / الملك العالم / العادل حسا / م الدين

Beneath rev. fleuron; muhmilah over حسا.

28. Copper. (British Museum. *Num. Chron.* no. 51.)

Same: but counterstamp, upside-down, upon the neck, نجم الدين.

The British Museum possesses a variety (*a*) which differs from (27) only in the addition of ·: over the م of العالم (*Num. Chron.* no. 52)—Pl. ii. cii.

The coins with the counterstamp نجم الدين are none the less to be attributed to Timurtásh because (as the stamp shows) they were in currency during Najm-ad-dín's reign. To attribute them to the latter would clearly be an error.

III. Najm-ad-dín Alpí. A.H. 547–572.

Type I.

29. Copper. (British Museum. *Num. Chron.* no. 53.)

Obv. Head as on preceding coins of Timurtásh; on neck نجم الدين, but not upside-down and not as a counterstamp, there being no sign of the edge of the punch such as is seen on the last two coins of Timurtásh.	Rev. ایل غازی / ملك الامرا / ابو المظفر / الپی بن

Beneath rev. fleuron. Muhmilah over ظ of المظفر and ب of first بن.

30. Copper. (Pl. ii. ciii.) (British Museum. *Num. Chron.* no. 55.)

Same: but, on the cheek, (shown by square edge of the punch), counterstamp, (nearly obliterating the name on the neck), نجم الدين ملك دياربكر.

It is evident that Najm-ad-dín at first used his father's coins, merely counterstamping them with his own name. When it became necessary to issue fresh money, he struck coins of the same type as those which he had been using; but he altered the reverse, by substituting his own name and titles for those of Timurtásh; and he also incorporated into the die of the obverse his own name, which before had only been counterstamped. He then appears to have made some acquisition to his territory, and to have commemorated the accession by putting on his coins a counterstamp which gives him the title of *King of Diyár-bakr.* After this he used other types than that of Timurtásh.

Type II.

31. Copper. (British Museum. *Num. Chron.* no. 57.)

OBV. نجم الدين

Two busts, diademed, face to face.

[Copied from coin of Gratian and Valentinian II.]

ملك دياربكر

REV. بن

تمرتاش بن ايل غازى بن

Two figures, standing, facing.

[Copied from coin of John II. Comnenus, representing the aureolate Virgin crowning the Emperor standing on her right, his right hand on his breast, his left holding the cross-bearing orb.]

ابو المظفر الپى

ارتق

Diacritical points to ش of تمرتاش.

The British Museum possesses two varieties (*Num. Chron.* nos. 58 and 59) of the coin just described, of which one is represented in Pl. ii. CIV. They both differ from (31) in writing اتق instead of ارتق. A further distinction between the three coins is to be observed: the first represents the cross (on the orb) by three points .·., the second by two :, the third by one.

I have put this type before the next, because I consider the simpler arrangement of its inscriptions, and their shortness, and the absence of any year of issue, as indications of an earlier date.

Type III.

1.

32. Copper. A.H. 558. (British Museum. *Num. Chron.* no. 60.)

OBV. A. Head, diademed, nearly facing.

M. الملك العالم العادل نجم الدين ملك دياربكر

REV. A. Bust, crowned, facing.

[The dress seems to be Byzantine.]

M. ابو المظفر الپى تمرتاش بن ايل غازى بن ارتق ثمان

Within marg. to dex. و خمسين

To sin. و خمسمائة

There are two varieties of this coin in the British Museum—(*a*) Pl. ii. CV. (*Num. Chron.* no. 61), same, but rev. marg. ابو المظفر الپى بن تمرتاش بن ايل غازى بن ارتق سنة; and within marg. to sin. ثمان وخمسين, to dex. وخمسمائة.—(*b*) (*Ibid.* no. 62), same as (*a*), but ثمان وخمسين and وخمسمائة are transposed and سنة is omitted.

2.

33. Copper. A.H. 559. (British Museum. *Num. Chron.* no. 64.)

Same as (32*b*): but تسع is substituted for ثمان and سنة is inserted.

Type IV.

34. Copper. (Pl. ii. cvi.) (British Museum. *Num. Chron.* no. 65.)

Obv. لا اله الا الله

امير المومنين | Two heads facing, slightly turned away one from the other. [A common Byzantine type.] | المستنجد بالله

محمد رسول الله

Rev. نجم الدين

ملك ديار بكر | Head facing, crowned, within small circle of dots. | ابن ارتق

البى بن ايل غازى

There are three varieties in the British Museum—(*a*) (*Num. Chron.* no. 68), same, except that المستنجد بالله and امير المومنين are transposed.—(*b*) (*Ibid.* no. 69), same as (34), but المستضى is substituted for المستنجد بالله and بامر الله for امير المومنين.—(*c*) (*Ibid.* no. 70), same as (34*a*), but المستضى is substituted for المستنجد بالله and بامر الله for امير المومنين.

The occurrence of the name of the Khalífah Al-Mustanjid limits the date of 34 and 34*a* to 555—566; whilst that of Al-Mustaḍí limits the date of 34*b* and 34*c* to 566—575. But it is clear that the *whole* of Type IV. must have followed Type III., for we cannot suppose that 34 and 34*a* were struck before 558, whilst 34*b* and 34*c* were struck after 566. Granting, then, that 34 and 34*a* were struck after Type III., *i.e.* after 559, their date is limited to 559—566. On the other hand, 34*b* and 34*c* must have been struck between the accession of Al-Mustaḍí and the death of Najm-ad-dín, *i.e.* between 566 and 572.

IV. Ḳuṭb-ad-dín Íl-Ghází II. A.H. 572–580.

Type I.

1.

35. Copper. A.H. 577. (British Museum. *Num. Chron.* no. 71.)

Obv. سبع وسبعين خمس
مائة

Two busts, diademed, facing; one larger than the other.
[Copied from coin of Heraklius I. and his son Heraklius Constantinus; but the Emperor's beard has been shaved, and the diadems have been much altered.]

Rev. قطب الدين بن
الناصر للدين
امير المومنين
هذا الدرهم
ملعون من لا
يغيره

(margins) نجم الدين بن | حسام الدين

Muhmilahs over امير and المومنين.

2.

36. Copper. A.H. 578. (British Museum. *Num. Chron.* no. 72.)

Same: but ثمان instead of سبع, and و inserted before خمس. No muhmilahs.

3.

37. Copper. A.H. 579. (British Museum. *Num. Chron.* no. 73.)

Same as (35): but تسع instead of سبع, and و omitted after تسع and after سبعين.

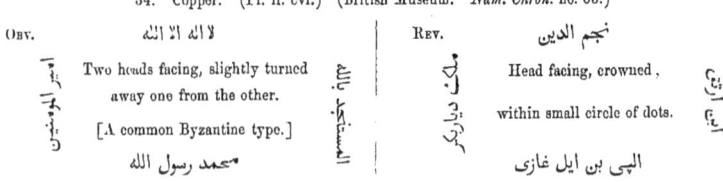

4.

38. Copper. A.H. 580. (British Museum. *Num. Chron.* no. 74.)

Same as (35): but ثمانين وخمس instead of سبع وسبعين خمس.
مائة مائة

5.

39. Copper. (British Museum. *Num. Chron.* no. 75.)

Same as (35): but سبع وثمان وخمس? instead of سبع وسبعين خمس (سبع = سبعين, with the unit and decimal transposed??). مائة مائة

6.

40. Copper. (Pl. vi. fig. 1.)[1] (British Museum. *Num. Chron.* no. 76.)

Same as (35): but ستة تسع تسعين وخمس? instead of سبع وسبعين خمس (سبعين = تسعين?).
مائة مائة

Point over اميز. Muhmilahs over المومنين and ملعون من.

I suspect that the dates of the last two coins are blundered. As they stand, they are undoubtedly incorrect.

On the curse-formula, which appears in its entirety on these coins (هذا الدرهم ملعون من يعيره), see above (*Introduction*, p. 9 and note, and no. 14 of the coins of the Kayfá dynasty).

The name of the Khalífah An-Náṣir has been the subject of a very common mistake among numismatists. Instead of the full surname *An-Náṣir-li-dini-lláh* اَلنَّاصِرُ لِدِينِ اللّٰهِ they have sometimes found (as on the coin just described) a form which they read *An-Náṣir-ad-dín*. This, I need scarcely say, is a solecism of a grave nature; and numismatists have made a great point of the ignorance or carelessness of those who had to do with the striking of the coins. It seemed to me highly improbable that any one entrusted with the designing or engraving of an Arabic coin should have been so ignorant of the Arabic language as to doubly define a noun; and I therefore thought it worth while to look into the matter a little more closely. The coins in the British Museum bearing the surname of the Khalífah An-Náṣir, about 250 in number, form quite large enough a collection to allow one to lay down general principles for the orthography of the name. By examining these 250 coins I found that what I had at first suspected was in fact correct—(i) in every instance of the supposed النَّاصِرُ آلدّين there was a connexion between the base of the (supposed) ا and the following ل of الدّين, thus showing the word to be للدّين; and (ii) consequently numismatists, ignorant or forgetful of the elementary rule of Arabic orthography, that the alif of the definitive *al*, when preceded by the preposition *li*, is elided, were unable to see the reason for the two láms occurring in juxtaposition, and accordingly attributed a solecism to the designers of the coin by reading En-Náṣir-ad-dín. After having investigated the question for myself, I discovered that Fraehn, with his usual accuracy, had already adopted the true reading النّاصر للدّين.

The correct form, then, of the contracted surname is اَلنَّاصِرُ لِلدِّينِ *An-Náṣir-li-d-dín*. In the full name the word دِين was defined by the following word اللّٰه; but that being removed in the contracted name, it became necessary to define دِين in some other way, and the definitive ال was accordingly prefixed, the resultant meaning being *to* THE *religion*, i.e. *Islám*, whereas لدين alone would mean *to* A *religion*.

[1] An indistinct specimen of this type is engraved on Pl. ii. fig. CVIII.

Type II.

41. Copper. (Pl. ii. fig. cxi.) (British Museum. *Num. Chron.* no. 77.)

Obv.	Rev.
بن الپی بن (left margin) ايل غازی Within dotted square, head to right, diademed. [Copied from coin of Constantine i.] (right margin) ارتق تمرتاش بن	ايل غازی لمولانـا الـمـالـكـ الـعـالـم الـعـادل قـطـب الـديـن مـلـكـ الامـرا شـاه دياربكر

There are some varieties in the incorrectness of the spelling of the word الملك—*e.g.* لماالك. On no example is it correctly spelt.

The unusual form [*Belonging*] *to our lord the king*, the assemblage of titles, and other peculiarities, induce the opinion that these coins were struck by some governor or chieftain tributary to the Urtuḳí Ḳuṭb-ad-dín.

V. Ḥusám-ad-dín Yúluḳ-Arslán. a.h. 580–597.

Type I.

1.

42. Copper. (Pl. ii. fig. cxii.) a.h. 581. (British Museum. *Num. Chron.* no. 85.)

Obv.	Rev.
Half-figure, right hand on breast. (left margin) ايل غازی بن [Probably copied from coin of Artavasdes and Nikephorus; but the robe is fastened in front, whereas the Byzantine is fastened on the right shoulder.] (right margin) حسام الدين يـ	Within hexagram of dotted lines, ايـوب الملكـ الناصر صلاح الدنيـا والديـن يوسف بن Between hexagram and outer dotted circle, ضرب | سنة | احد | ثمانيـ(*sic*) | خمس | مائة

2.

43. Copper. (*Silvered.*)[1] a.h. 581. (British Museum. *Num. Chron.* no. 83.)

Same: but different obv. inscription, and differently divided: حسام الدين \| يولق ارسلان.

3.

44. Copper. a.h. 583. (British Museum. *Num. Chron.* no. 86.)

Same as (43): but ثلث instead of احد.

[1] A duplicate of this coin in the British Museum (*Num. Chron.* no. 84) is similarly *silvered.*

4.

45. Copper. A.H. 584. (British Museum. *Num. Chron.* no. 87.)

Same as (43): but اربع instead of احد.

5.

46. Copper. A.H. 585. (British Museum. *Num. Chron.* no. 89.)

Same as (43): but خمس instead of احد.

Pietraszewski (*Num. Muh.* no. 264) publishes a coin (*a*) which resembles (43) in everything but the date, which is 586 (ست instead of احد).

It has already been noticed (cp. no. 16) that the name of Ṣaláḥ-ad-dín as liege-lord occurs on the coinage both of Kayfá and of Máridín in this same year 581.

Type II.

47. Copper. (Pl. vi. fig. 2.) A.H. 587–9. (British Museum. *Num. Chron.* no. 90.)

OBV. حسام الدين ملك دياربكر

Two heads: that on the right, profile to left; that on the left, smaller, nearly facing, crowned.
[The profile is probably copied from a coin of Nero; but the head on the left is clearly Byzantine:—apparently a mixed type.]

REV. الملك الناصر
صلاح الدين
محيى دولة
امير المومنين

In left margin: بن ايوب; in right margin: يوسف

Above, fleuron.

Over صلاح on rev., muhmilah.

Three other examples in the British Museum differ slightly from (47):—(*a*) omitting the fleuron and the muhmilah; (*b*) *gilt*, substituting a pellet for the fleuron, and retaining the muhmilah; (*c*) transposing يوسف and بن ايوب, substituting pellet for fleuron (like *b*), and retaining muhmilah.

We can scarcely suppose that this type was issued before the last coin (46*a*) of Type I. was struck; the *terminus a quo* of the date is thus fixed at 586. But it is probable that, in the absence of political changes which might necessitate an alteration in the coinage,—and we have no knowledge of such changes in this instance,—a fresh coinage would not be issued till the former one was exhausted, for which we may allow a year. Hence we may fix the earliest date at which Type II. was likely to be struck at the year 587. The *terminus ad quem* is easily seen to be 589; for the name of Ṣaláḥ-ad-dín occurs on the coin, and he died in 589. Further, a new type of coinage (Type III.) was introduced by Yúluḳ-Arslán in 589. There remains therefore the narrow range of between two and three years (587, 588, and part of 589) during which Type II. must have been struck.

Type III.

1.

48. Copper. A.H. 589. (British Museum. *Num. Chron.* no. 94.)

OBV. Four full figures: one is seated in the midst, with head dejected; behind stands another, with face in profile and right arm upraised; two other figures stand one on each side of the sitting one, the figure to dexter with arms raised, that to sinister with arms down.

REV. A. الامام النـــا
صر للـديـــن
امير المومنين

M. حسام الدين ملك ديار بكر يولق ارسلان
بن ايل غازى بن ا[ر]تق تسع وثمانين وخمسمائة

Of two varieties in the British Museum (*Num. Chron.* nos. 95, 96):—(*a*) (Pl. iii. fig. cxv) differs from (48) in having a star before the sitting figure, and inserting سنة before تسع and ر in ارتق; (*b*) is similar to (*a*), but omits the star, and adds annulets, one on each side and one a-top of rev. area, and also inserts a muhmilah over صر.

2.

49. Copper. A.H. 589. (British Museum. *Num. Chron.* no. 97.)

OBV. Same as (48): but no star, and slight alterations in the figures, outer drapery being added to the side figures.

REV. A. الملك العادل
الامام النـــا
صر لـلديـــن
امير المومنين
سيف الديـن
ابو بكر | بن ايوب

Fleuron.

M. Same as on (48), but ر inserted in ارتق, سنة before تسع, and the century of the date illegible.

Two other examples in the British Museum slightly differ from (49):—(*a*) (*Num. Chron.* no. 98) is stamped with a countermark GG (inverted); (*b*) (*Ibid.* no. 99) *silvered*, omits the fleuron on rev. area.

3.

50. Copper. A.H. 590. (British Museum. *Num. Chron.* no. 100.)

Same as (49): but date تسعين وخمسمائة instead of تسع وثمانين وخمسمائة.

A variety in the British Museum (*Num. Chron.* no. 101) adds a pellet under rev. area.

It has been suggested that this group is intended to record the lamentation of the Muslims on the occasion of the death in the year 589 of their great champion Ṣaláḥ-ad-dín, who had so long led their triumphant armies against the infidel Franks. This is by no means disproved by Dr. Scott's discovery (*Revue Archéologique*, x. 296) that the representation on these coins bears a strong resemblance to a relief in terra-cotta (in the British Museum) representing the mourning of Penelope for the absent Odysseus. The Urtuḳís may have been anxious to engrave on their coins some mark of their regret (whether sincere or merely politic) for the death of the great Saracen leader, and they found a suitable model in the relief above mentioned, of which they may very possibly have seen an example.

Type IV.

1.

51. Copper. A.H. 596. (British Museum. *Num. Chron.* no. 102.)

Obv. Helmeted figure, seated cross-legged; holding, in right hand, sword horizontally behind his head; in left hand, a trunkless, helmeted, head, by the plume of the helmet; handle of sword crossed, tasselled. To dex., stem with three buds. Beneath figure, fleuron.	Rev. A. الناصر لديـن الله اميــــر المومنيــــن M. (Inner). الملك الافضل على والملك الظاهر غازى بن الملك الناصر (Outer). حسام الدين يولق ارسلان ايل غازى بن [ا]رتق ضرب سنة ست وتسعين وخمسمائة

2.

52. Copper. A.H. 596. (British Museum. *Num. Chron.* no. 103.)

Same: but ملك دياربكر بن inserted between ارسلان and ايل غازى, and ا inserted in ارتق.

3.

53. Copper. A.H. 596. (British Museum. *Num. Chron.* no. 104.)

Same as (51): but on obv. to dex. (instead of stem with buds) the words written sideways نور الدين اتا / بك. Also on rev. area muhmilah over the ص of الناصر. Rev. marg. as on (51), but date stops at تسعـ.

4.

54. Copper. (Pl. iii. fig. cxx.) A.H. 596. (British Museum. *Num. Chron.* no. 105.)

Same as (53): but with ملك دياربكر بن inserted as on (52).

A variety (*a*) in the British Museum (*Num. Chron.* no. 106) omits the muhmilah over the ص of الناصر.

5.

55. Copper. A.H. 596. (British Museum. *Num. Chron.* no. 108.)

Same as (53): but obverse type *reversed*; sword in left hand, trunkless head in right, etc. Pellet above rev. area.

6.

56. Copper. A.H. 596. (British Museum. *Num. Chron.* no. 109.)

Same as (55): but stem of buds restored in place of side-inscription.	Rev. A. الـلـه الامام الـنـــا صرلـــديـــن امير المومنين

The supposition that this type refers to a scene which took place in the tent of Ṣaláḥ-ad-dín (Abú-l-Fidá, ann. 582) appears to me improbable, as the event took place fourteen years and the principal actor died seven years before the coin was struck.[1]

[1] Before leaving the coins of Yúluḳ-Arslán, I must mention that Soret (*3e Lettre*, no. 59, *Rev. Num. Belge*, iv. 36, 2nde série) attributes to this prince a silver coin which I have no hesitation in asserting should properly be assigned to Aẓ-Ẓáhir Ghází, the Ayyúbí prince of Ḥalab. The word Soret reads يولق should be يوسف, and ارسلان should be غازى.

VI. Násir-ad-dín Urtuk-Arslán. A.H. 597–637.

Type I.

1.

57. Copper. A.H. 598. (British Museum. *Num. Chron.* no. 110.)

Obv. Bust, facing; on each side, star. (right) ناصر الدين (left) ارتق ارسلان

Rev. A. Within hexagram,

الله
الامام الناصر
لدين امير المو
منين

M. In the spaces between hexagram and double dotted outer circle,

ضرب | سنة | ثمان | تسعين | خمس | مائة

2.

58. Copper. (Pl. vi. fig. 3.) A.H. 599. (British Museum. *Num. Chron.* no. 111.)

Obv. Same.

Rev. A. Within hexagram,[1]

الله
الامام الناصر
لدين امير المومنين
الملك الظاهر
غازى

M. ضرب | سنة | تسع | تسعين | وخمس | مائة

Another specimen (*a*) in the British Museum differs from (58) only in dividing ار | تق instead of ا | رتق, and in offering some obscurity in part of the date, owing to the indifferent preservation of the coin. A third example (*b*) substitutes for ناصر الدين | ا رتق | ا رسلان the words الملك المظفر | ارتق | ارسلان, of which الملك is somewhat obscured by having a hole pierced through it. This last piece presents the peculiarity of having its present inscriptions and head struck over those of another coin, which must, of course, have been issued at an earlier date. To this earlier coin must be assigned the words الملك المظفر which have obscured the name ناصر الدين on the obverse. On the reverse, the inscriptions of Urtuk-Arslán's die are nearly obliterated, whilst those of the earlier die are more than half legible:—

سنة اربع
الناصر لدين الله
. . . منين
. . . لناصر
. . .

(margin) المومنين

This inscription clearly indicates the date 584; and the earlier die may be attributed without hesitation to

[1] A distinction may be noted between this and the preceding hexagram. That of (57) is triple, being formed by two hexagrams of single lines, inclosing one of dots. The hexagram of (58), on the other hand, is composed of the two lines without the dots, as in the photographic representation on Pl. vi.

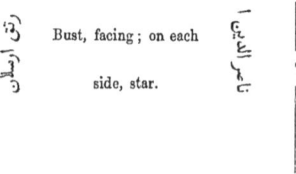

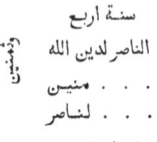

Al-Malik Al-Muẓaffar Sinjar-Sháh, the Atábég of Al-Jazírah, as a comparison with the coins of that prince clearly shows. It may perhaps seem strange that the earlier inscription should be preserved whilst the later inscription struck over it has almost disappeared; but this may perhaps be accounted for by supposing that the later inscription preserved the older one by undergoing the wear of circulation which would otherwise have fallen upon it. There can be no doubt whatever that the die of Urtuḳ-Arslán is the super-imposed one: this is proved not only by the date of the other die, but by the nature of the surface of the copper, which renders it usually an easy task to determine which of two dies struck on the same place is the older one.

The word الله at the top of the reverse of the preceding four coins must be taken with الناصر لدين. Its unusual position, separated from its connected words, is, we may suppose, due to an attempt at symmetry.

Type II.

1.

59. Copper. (Pl. iii. fig. cxxiv.) A.H. 599. (British Museum. *Num. Chron.* no. 114.)

Obv. Crowned or helmeted centaur-archer [Sagittarius] to left, head turned facing, stretching with right hand the string of a bow which he holds in the left, with the intent of shooting down the throat of a dragon with jaws a-gape. The dragon is nothing else than an extension of the centaur's tail. To the left of the centaur's head is a large point.

In the spaces round the figure,

بماردين | سنة | تسع | تسعين و | خمسه | ما

Rev.

بن ايوب

الناصر لدين الله امير

المومنين الملك

العادل ابو بكر

ملك دياربكر

سلان

(left side) ارتق ار — (right side) ناصر الدين

The first component of the numeral خمسمائة on this coin is reversed (سمخ); and the second, though not reversed, is curtailed to ما.

A variety (*a*) in the British Museum (*Num. Chron.* no. 115) differs from (59) in that نا (of ناصر) is removed from the right side to the same line as دياربكر, thus ملك دياربكر نا. A third example (*b*) (*Num. Chron.* no. 116) is similar to (*a*), but سمخ is changed to خمس and و inserted after تسع. A fourth (*c*) (*Num. Chron.* no. 117) is like (*b*), except that نا of ناصر is at the side as on (59).

2.

60. Copper. A.H. 599. (British Museum. *Num. Chron.* no. 118.)

Same as (59), but the centaur-archer is reversed, to right, bow in right hand, string stretched with left; and the obv. inscription is thus distributed in the spaces—بماردين سـ | نة | تسع و تسعـ | ين و | خمس | مائة; and on the rev. نا is moved to the line of ملك دياربكر as on (59*a*).

Of two varieties of this coin (*Num. Chron.* nos. 120, 121) in the British Museum, the first (*a*) divides the obv. inscription thus, بماردين | سنة | تسعين | و | تسع وخمس مائة; and the second (*b*) thus, بماردين | تسعين و | تسع | وخمسمائة سنة, neither of which arrangements in the least affects the meaning of the date: (*a*) places نا of ناصر as on (59), but (*b*) as on (59*a*).

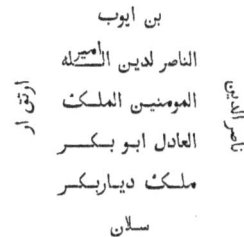

The patronymic بن ايوب on the rev. belongs of course to the Ayyúbí Al-Malik Al-'Ádil Abú-Bakr, not to Náṣir-ad-dín Urtuḳ-Arslán, although at first sight it might seem from its position to be a continuation of the latter name.[1]

It is perhaps noteworthy that the piece (no. 59) struck by Urtuḳ-Arslán at Máridín in the year 598 is the earliest instance of a coin of the princes of Máridín bearing a mint-name: their Kayfá kinsmen introduced *Al-Ḥiṣn* twenty years earlier (see no. 14).

Type III.

61. Copper. (Pl. iii. fig. cxxxi.) Máridín. A.H. 606. (British Museum. *Num. Chron.* no. 123.)

Obv. A. Man seated on lion to left, hands raised, ends of girdle flying behind.	Rev. A. وست الامام النـاصر (right margin) ستّ لدين الله امير مائة (left margin) المومنين
M. الملك العالم العادل ناصر الدين ارتق ارسلان ملك دياربكر	M. الملك العادل سيف الدين ابو بكر ابن ايوب ضرب بماردين سنة

Of two trifling varieties in the British Museum, (*a*) differs as to the obv. margin, which stops at ديار, and as to the rev. margin, where بن is substituted for ابن; whilst (*b*) omits ضرب in rev. margin, and inserts a fleuron above the lowest line of rev. area. (*Num. Chron.* 125, 126.)

A duplicate of (61) in the same collection is plated with *silver*.

The expression سنة ستة, though ungrammatical, is by no means a unique solecism: similar mistakes are not uncommon on coins.

Type IV.

1.

62. Copper. (Pl. iii. fig. cxxxvi.) A.H. 611. (British Museum. *Num. Chron.* no. 127.)

Obv. A. Head, laureate, facing (slightly turned to left).	Rev. * ⩡ * [2] ابو العباس احمــد (right margin) احدى عشر الناصر لدين الـلـه امير المو ا منين وستمائة (left margin) الملك العادل ابو (بكر بن ايوب)
M. ناصر الدنيا والدين ارتق ارسلان ملك دياربكر	

(The words in parentheses are inserted from duplicate specimens.)

[1] It is a graceless office to comment on the mistakes of those scholars who formerly directed their labours to the same field as myself, but I cannot forbear to mention that in describing the preceding coin (in Eichhorn's *Repertorium*, x. 13. 23), Reiske seems to have tried to make as many egregious blunders as he possibly could. Certain it is that scarcely a line but offers a tempting subject for criticism. Whether Reiske was an Arabic scholar or not, though a sufficiently dubitable question, is not one with which we are at present concerned; but that he was no Arabic numismatist is a patent fact, and every numismatic statement or theory of his demands the most cautious scrutiny.

[2] Some numismatists, with singular infelicity, have read the top line امر الفلس احمد, and the engraving in Pl. iii. is likely to confirm this mistake. I need only say that the coins unanimously give the reading ابو العباس احمد, the names of the Khalífah An-Náṣir, and that the other reading is not only unauthorized but ungrammatical.

Another specimen (*a*) has annulets instead of stars above rev. (*Num. Chron.* no. 129). The photograph (Pl. vi. fig. 4) will convey a better impression of the obverse than the engraving.

2.

63. Copper. A.H. 611. (British Museum. *Num. Chron.* no. 132.)

OBV. Head as before, but slightly turned to *right*.

Some illegible characters in the margin.

REV.

. . . . . .

الملك الكامل

محمد بن ايوب

الملك المنصور

ناصر الدين ارتق

(ارسلان)

(margins: الامام — الناصر)

Type V.

64. Copper. A.H. 615. (British Museum. *Num. Chron.* no. 135.)

OBV. Within octogram,

•

الناصر لدين الله

امير

• المومنين الملك •

الكامل محمد

•

Between octogram and outer double circle,

لا | اله | الا | (الله) | (محمد | رسو | ل ال) | له

REV. Within octogram,

•

ناصر

الملك المنصور

• الدنيا والدين •

ارتق ارسلان

•

Between octogram and outer double circle,

(ضر) | ب | سنة | خمس | عشر | ... | ... | ...

Another example in the British Museum (*Num. Chron.*, no. 137) is struck over a coin of Type IV.

Type VI.

65. Copper. (Pl. vi. fig. 5.) A.H. 620. (British Museum. *Num. Chron.* no. 138.)

OBV. A. Head to right.

[Copied from coin of Nero.]

M. الملك المنصور ناصر الدنيا والدين ارتق ارسلان

REV.

عشرين

الناصر لدين الله

امير المومنين

الملك الكامل

ناصر الدين محمد

بن ايوب

(margins: ضرب سنة — وستمائة)

Fleuron over المومنين.

Type VII.

66. Copper. (Pl. vi. fig. 6.) A.H. 623. (British Museum. *Num. Chron.* no. 140.)

Obv. A. Bust facing, with long locks of hair.

M. السلطان الاعظم علا الدين كيقباد بن كيـ

On left side of head, خسـ } = خسرو
On right side of head, رو

Rev.

وعشرين و
الامام
المستنصر بالله
امير المومنين
الملك المنصور
ارتق

The British Museum possesses two varieties of this type besides that just described (*Num. Chron.* nos. 141, 142): of these (*a*) is noteworthy only because the obv. is struck over a rev. of Type VI., and the rev. over an obv. of Type VI.; and (*b*) differs from (66) in having two muhmilahs (٧), one over المومنين, the other over المنصور, taking the place of the ر, which is on this coin (unlike the preceding) written in line with the rest of the word.

Type VIII.

1.

67. Silver. (Pl. vi. fig. 7.) Dunaysir. A.H. 625. (British Museum. *Num. Chron.* no. 143.)

Obv.

بالله
الامام المستنصر
* * *
ارتق
الملك المنصور

Rev.

بدنيسر سنة
السلطان المعظم
كيقباد بن كيخسرو

The points on this coin are diacritical: viz. obv. المستنصر عشرين, rev. المغظم كيقباد بن كيخسرو. A variety (*a*) in the same collection (*Num. Chron.* no. 144) differs only in omitting the points over the خ and the ن.

2.

68. Silver. Dunaysir. A.H. 626. (British Museum.)[1]

Same as (67), but ستة instead of خمس on obv. Points as on (67*a*), but none to المستنصر.

3.

69. Silver. Dunaysir. A.H. 628. (Faba Collection, no. 440.)[2]

Same as (67), but ثمان instead of خمس on obv.

[1] Cp. Fraehn, *Recensio*, cl. xiii. 11.

[2] I am indebted to Dr. Blau for a description of this piece.

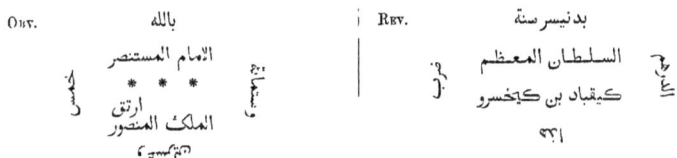

4.

70. Silver. Dunaysir. A.H. 632. (British Museum. *Inedited.*)

Same as (67), but وثلثين | اثنين instead of وعشرين | خمس.

Points—obv. المستنصر; rev. المعظم كيقباذ بن. Star over كيقباد.

These silver coins—the first in the Urtuḳí series—are precisely after the model of those issued by the Saljúḳí Sulṭáns of Anatolia: the size, the peculiar ornamentation with three stars, the arrangement of the inscriptions, the style of the writing, all are Saljúḳí. In explanation of this, we see the name of Kay-Ḳubád on the reverse, showing that at the time these coins were struck the Urtuḳí prince was doing homage to the Saljúḳí Sulṭán. The acknowledgment of suzerainty seems to have been accompanied by a change in the coinage in imitation of that of the suzerain. In the like manner, a little later, we see the same Urtuḳí prince copying the well-known type of coinage peculiar to the Ayyúbí princes.

Type IX.

1.

71. Copper. A.H. 626. (British Museum. *Num. Chron.* no. 147.)

Obv.	Rev.
Man seated on lion, similar to Type III.	ضرب سنة المستنصر بالله امير المومنين (ستة وعشرين)

Circular marginal inscription on obv. and rev., but nearly effaced and quite illegible.

2.

72. Copper. A.H. 627. (Müller Collection.)[1]

Same as (71), but سبع عشرين instead of ستة وعشرين.

Type X.

73. Silver. A.H. 628. (British Museum. *Num. Chron.* no. 150.)

Obv.	Rev.
A. Within triple hexagram composed of a dotted line between two plain lines, الامام المستنصر بالله امير المو منين	A. Within hexagram (as on obv.), محمد الملك الكامل الملك المنصور ارتق
M. In spaces between hexagram and triple circle similarly composed, لا اله | (الا ا) لله) | محمد رسول | الله	M. In spaces between hexagram and circle (as on obv.), (ضرب) | بكيفا | سنة | ثمان ٥ | ٥ عشرين | وستمائة

(The words in parentheses are, as before, inserted from other examples.)

[1] Formerly belonging to Dr. O. Blau, German Consul-General at Odessa.

Dr. Blau mentions to me a similar dirham formerly in his possession, bearing the date 625 خمس وعشرين وستمائة. Can this be a misreading for 628 ثمان وعشرين وستمائة? At least, of the reading of the coin described above I have no doubt.

The photograph (Pl. vi. fig. 8) is taken from a second specimen in the British Museum.

This type of coinage is an exact copy of that characteristic of the Ayyúbís, and seems to have been adopted in token of homage, in the like manner as Type VIII. appears to have been adopted in honour of the Saljúkís.

Type XI.

74. Copper. (Pl. vi. fig. 9.) A.H. 628. (British Museum. *Num. Chron.* no. 154.)

Obv. Figure seated cross-legged, within square of dotted lines, head projecting above square; star on each side of head; annulets on each side of figure within square.

Margin: ناصر الدين — ارتق ارسلان

|| ≚ ||

Rev.

بالله
الامام المستنصر
امير المومنين
الملك الكامل
محمد

Margin: ضرب سنة ثمان — وعشرين وستمائة

Another example (*a*) in the same collection differs only in transposing ناصر الدين and ارتق ارسلان.

Type XII.

75. Copper. Máridín. A.H. 634. (British Museum. *Num. Chron.* no. 157.)

Obv. A. Head to face, diademed, similar to Type VII., but broader.

M. السلطان المعظم علا الدنيا والدين كيقباد
قسيم امير المومنين

Rev.

ضرب بماردين
الامام
المستنصر بالله
* * *
امير المومنين
الملك المنصور
ارتق

Margin: ثلثين وستمائة — سنة اربع

A variety (*a*) in the British Museum divides the date thus وستمائة | وثلثين [اربع] and omits كيقباد in obv. margin (*Num. Chron.* no. 159); and a third (*b*) omits المومنين in obv. margin, and turns the date round, beginning at left instead of top, وستمائة | وثلثين ؟ اربع | سنة | [ضرب . . . ؟].

The engraving (Pl. iii. fig. CXLIV) is from a considerably less perfect specimen than that described above (75).

Type XIII.

76. Copper. Máridín. A.H. 634. (British Museum. *Num. Chron.* no. 161.)

OBV. A. Figure seated, cross-legged, holding orb in left hand.

M. السلطان المعظم غياث الدين كيخسرو
قسيم امير المومنين

REV. (ضرب) بماردين
الامام
المستنصر بالله
امير المومنين
الملك المنصور
ارتق

Margins: سنة اربع و (ثلثين ستمائة)

The British Museum possesses eight specimens of this type, differing only (so far as can be seen) in degree of indistinctness. It is from a comparison with the other seven pieces that the words in parentheses have been inserted. One of the eight is struck over Type VI. (obv. over obv., rev. over rev.). From another of these eight pieces, the representation in Pl. vi. fig. 10 is taken.

The decimal of the date on these coins is so very obscure that there might be some uncertainty as to whether the year were 604, 614, 624, or 634, if it were not for the circumstance that one of them is struck over a die of Type VI. Now Type VI. was issued in 620, and Type XIII. must therefore have been issued later than 620. But the name of Kay-Khusrú occurs on it. This cannot be Kay-Khusrú I., for he reigned from 600 to 607, whereas it has already been shown that Type XIII. must have been issued later than 620. The alternative, Kay-Khusrú II., began to reign in 634. The date of Type XIII. must therefore be 634. A later decad is precluded by the death of Urtuḳ-Arslán in 637.

Type XIV.

77. Copper. (British Museum. *Num. Chron.* no. 169.)

OBV. الامام الناصر
لدين الله امير [المو
منين]

REV. [محمد]
الملك العزيز
الملك المنصور
[ارتق]

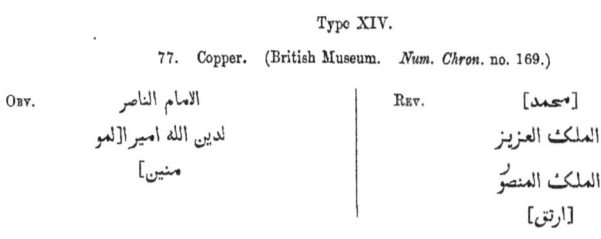

VII. Najm-ad-dín Ghází. A.H. 637–658.

Type I.

78. Copper. A.H. 640—3. (Soret, *IVe Lettre*, no. 100, *Rev. Num. Belge*, 2e sér. ii. 222.)

Obv. Within square,

السلطان المـ . .
غياث الدين الملك
السعيد نجم الدين

Rev. Within square,

الامام ا
لمستعصم
بالله امير المو

Traces of marginal inscriptions.

The date of this coin is limited to 640—3 by the accession of Al-Musta'ṣim in 640 and the death of Ghiyáth-ad-dín (Kay-Khusrú II.) in 643.

Type II.

79. Copper. A.H. 646? (British Museum. *Num. Chron.* no. 170.)

Obv. A.

بالله
الامام المستعصم
امير المومنين

M. (الله محمد رسول الله) . . . .

Rev. A.

الملك الصالح
نجم الدين ايوب الملك
السعيد غازى
بن ارتق

M. . . (ست واربعين وستما ؟) . . . . . .

(The words in parentheses are inserted from another specimen in the same collection.)

In the late General Bartholomaei's *IVe Lettre à M. Soret* (*Rev. Num. Belge*, ii. 340, 4e série) is a description (no. 25) of a coin resembling the preceding, but with date 645 and a different reverse inscription.

Type III.

80. Copper. (Pl. vi. fig. 11.) Máridín. A.H. 654. (British Museum. *Num. Chron.* no. 172.)

Obv. A. Head, facing.

M. الامام المستعصم بالله امير المومنين

Above, two stars.

Rev. Within dotted square.

• يوسف •
الملك الناصر
الملك السعيد
• غازى •

In the spaces between square and outer dotted circle,

ضرب بماردين | سنة | اربع وا | خمسين ستمائة

Type IV.

1.

81. Silver. (Pl. vi. fig. 12.) Máridín. A.H. 655. (British Museum. *Num. Chron.* no. 174.)

OBV. Within triple hexagram composed of dotted line between two plain lines,

الامام

المستعصم

بالله اميرالمو

منين

In spaces between hexagram and outer circle similarly composed,

لا اله | الا ا | لله | محمد | رسول | الله

REV. Within hexagram (as on obv.),

يوسف

الملك الناصر

الملك السعيد

غازى

In spaces (as on obv.),

(ضرب) | بماردين | سنة | خمس و | خمسين | (وستمائة)

2.

82. Silver. Máridín. A.H. 656. (British Museum. *Num. Chron.* no. 176.)

OBV. In hexagram (as before),

الله

لا اله الا

الله محمد

رسول

In spaces (as before),

صلى | الله | عليه | وعلى | اله | وسلم

REV. As on (81), but ست instead of خمس.

The rev. marg. inscription has been made out by comparison with other specimens.

3.

83. Silver. Máridín. A.H. 657. (British Museum. *Num. Chron.* no. 177.)

Same as (82), but سبع (or rather سع, it might perhaps be تسع) instead of ست.

4.

84. Silver. Máridín. A.H. 658. (Bartholomaei, *IVe Lettre*, no. 26, *Rev. Num. Belge*, 4e sér. ii.)

Same as (82), but ثمان instead of ست.

The reason for the alteration of the obverse inscription and for the omission of the Khalífah's name is to be found in the fact that Al-Musta'ṣim, the last of the Khalífahs of Baghdád, was murdered by Húlágú in 656.

VIII. Ḳará-Arslán. A.H. 658–691.

Type I.

85. Silver. (Pietraszewski, *Num. Muh.* 308.)

Obv. A. Within hexagram (as on 81).	Rev. A. Within hexagram (as on 81).
هولاگو	الملك المظفر
المعظم	قــــر ارســـــلان
ب	

Marginal inscriptions nearly effaced.

Pietraszewski wrongly attributed this coin to Ḳilij-Arslán, the Saljúḳí Sulṭán of Ar-Rúm.

Type II.

86. Copper. (Pl. vi. fig. 13.) (British Museum. *Num. Chron.* no. 179.)

Obv. A.	Rev. A.
هولاگو	الملــك
المعظم	المــظــفر
	قر ارسلان
M. Illegible.	M. Illegible.

Another example (*a*) has V beneath obv. area.

IX. Shams-ad-dín Dáwúd. A.H. 691–693.

Type I.

87. Copper. (Vienna Museum. Fraehn, *Bull. Scient.* ii. 1837, p. 177; Krafft, *Wellenheim Cat.* 12273; engraved in Lelewel, *Numismatique du Moyen-Age*, Atlas, title-page.)

Obv.	Rev.
Christ, seated on throne;	الملك العا . .
similar to Type VI. of	العادل شمس
Ḳará-Arslán of Kayfá.	الدنيا والدين

It must be admitted that this is only a conjectural attribution. The titles and style of the coin lead one to the supposition that it was issued by Shams-ad-dín Dáwúd the Urtuḳí; but the evidence is anything but certain. In the absence, however, of a more positive attribution, we may provisionally assign it to the Urtuḳí prince.

APPENDIX A.

TURKISH NAMES.

In writing Turkish names I have adopted the orthography of the Arabic historians, some of whom were contemporaries of the princes who bore these names and may therefore be supposed to have known how they were pronounced. As, however, this orthography differs considerably from the Turkish, I insert below a list of the names as given by Mr. J. W. Redhouse, who has kindly furnished me with the Turkish orthography and probable meaning of each word.

أورتوق ارسلان = *covered* or *hairy lion.*[1]

يولوق ارسلان = *plucked* or *bald lion.*[2]

قرا ارسلان = *black lion.*

سوقمان = *an overboot*; but

سگمان (Pers.) = *dog-like*; or perhaps

سگبان (Pers.) = *an attendant on hounds.*

تيمورتاش = *iron-stone*, or perhaps [one's] *companion-in-iron.*

الپى = probably *one who has served under Alp-Arslán*, a *follower of Alp-Arslán.*

إيل غازى = *hand-victor*, or *tribe-conqueror*. The significations of the Turkish إيل are too numerous to enable one to determine with certainty the meaning of the name. غازى is Arabic.

APPENDIX B.

PALÆOGRAPHY.

The style of Arabic writing employed by the Urtuḳís on their coins was of a mixed nature. The old rigidly-simple Kúfí character was passing away, and the transitional Kúfí was preparing the road for the Naskhí. We find all three kinds on Urtuḳí coins. A few present the old Kúfí in very nearly its pristine simplicity, a few on the other hand the Naskhí in almost its modern form, but the majority employ the transitional Kúfí, in which the simplicity of the old character is destroyed by the addition of ornamental turns and other embellishments. All this may be seen at once by a glance at the plates.

Diacritical points are very sparingly used on these coins. The following are all I have met with: فخر الدين, معين امير المومنس, المستنجد, ستس, سكمان, بن, بن, قرا ارسلان, خمسمايه, في سنه, سنه, المغطم, كيقباد, كيقباد, كيخسرو, تمرتاش, عشر, المومنس. Of orthographical signs, *shaddah* occurs once (الدّين), and *ihmál* (or *muhmilah*, as de Sacy calls it) frequently (v). When employed in grammatical works, *ihmál* shows that a letter is *pointless*; but on the coins, though it is generally used in this manner, it is not always. The examples of its occurrence furnished by the Urtuḳí coinage are: فخر, العادل, العالم,

1 أورتوق from أورتمق to *cover, envelop, veil.*

2 يولوق from يولمق to *pluck* (hairs or feathers).

المصوّر, الناصّر, ضّلاح, ملعوّن مّن, امىّر المومنّس, نّن, المطّفر, محموّد, الضّالّح, المّلكّ, كىحسّرو. Of these the *ihmál* over the ع s of العالم and العادل is clearly to show that they are not غ s. Similarly كيخسرو is shown not to be كيخشرو, الصالح not الضالح, صلاح not ضلاح, الناصر not الناضر. But the *ihmál* over the م of العالم, الملك, seems useless, for there is no risk of confusing م with any dotted letter; unless, indeed, on a badly-engraved coin it could be mistaken for ـغـ or ـڠـ in the middle of a word. On the other hand, the *ihmál* over the خ of فخر is not only incorrect but is contradicted by the coin itself, for the خ is in this instance pointed. So again *ihmál* over the ظ of المظفر is incorrect. It appears to me that whilst this sign was commonly used on the coins to indicate that the letter was *muhmalah* or pointless, it was also sometimes used merely as an ornament. There is nothing else relating to the Arabic palæography of these coins which cannot be learnt from the autotype plates.

APPENDIX C.

ASTROLOGICAL TYPES.

Many of the types on the coins described in the preceding pages have been shown to be copies of Byzantine or Seleucid or Roman originals; but many have been left unidentified. Of these I am now in a position to prove that some are *astrological.* Dr. E. von Bergmann lately called my attention to the astrological character of some of the Urtukí types, and referred me to a plate at the end of Reinaud's *Monuments Arabes etc. du cabinet de M. le duc de Blacas.* This engraving represents an astrological mirror, belonging to an Urtukí prince, Núr-ad-dín Urtuk-Sháh, great-grandson of Abú-Bakr I. of Khartapirt. One side of this mirror is of course polished; but on the other, besides inscriptions, are two zones or bands, of which the inner contains seven busts representing the planets, and the outer twelve medallions inclosing figures representing the signs of the Zodiac combined with the seven planets. 'Chaque planète a un signe du zodiaque qu'elle affectionne de prédilection et dont elle se rapproche autant qu'il est possible: plus elle est près de ce signe, plus elle conserve d'influence; plus elle s'en éloigne, plus elle s'affaiblit. . . . La planète au reste domine toujours, et la signe est entièrement sous sa dépendance' (Reinaud, ii. 408 ff.). Cancer is under the dominion of the Moon, Leo of the Sun, Virgo of Mercury, Libra of Venus, Scorpio of Mars, Sagittarius of Jupiter, Capricornus of Saturn. But as there are twelve zodiacal signs and only seven planets (in this system) the remaining five signs are distributed to the planets again, beginning with the last: Saturn has Aquarius, Jupiter Pisces, Mars Aries, Venus Taurus, Mercury Gemini.

This curious mirror throws light on more than one of the unexplained Urtukí types. Mars in Aries is represented by a man seated on a ram, holding in one hand a sword and in the other a trunkless head. There can be no doubt, therefore, that Type VI. of Yúluk-Arslán, which represents a similar figure, though without the ram, is intended for the planet Mars. Again, Type II. of Urtuk-Arslán is clearly meant for Sagittarius, and exactly corresponds to the representation of that sign on the astrological mirror: Jupiter, to whom the sign Sagittarius belongs, being sufficiently represented by the man-element in the figure. In a similar manner we shall be able in a future part of the *Numismata Orientalia* to explain some of the astrological types which occur on the coins of the Atábégs.

STEPHEN AUSTIN AND SONS, PRINTERS, HERTFORD.

URTUKIS of KAYFA.

CXLVII.

C.

562.

CLIII.

C.

571.

CLIV.

C.

581–97.

CLV.

C.

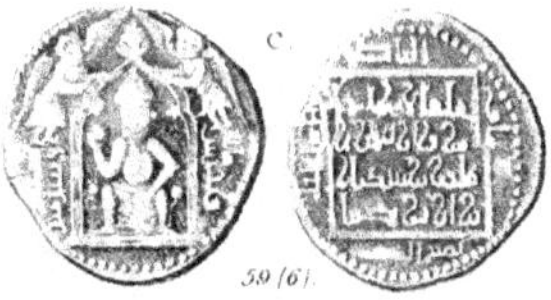

59 (6).

CLVIII.

C.

617.

CLIX.

C.

618–22.

URTUKIS of MARIDIN.

CII.

C.

516–47.

CIII.

C.

547–72.

CIV.

C.

547–80.

CV.

C.

558.

Vincent Brooks Day & Son Lith

URTUKIS of MARIDIN

CVI.
C.

555-66.

CVIII.
C.

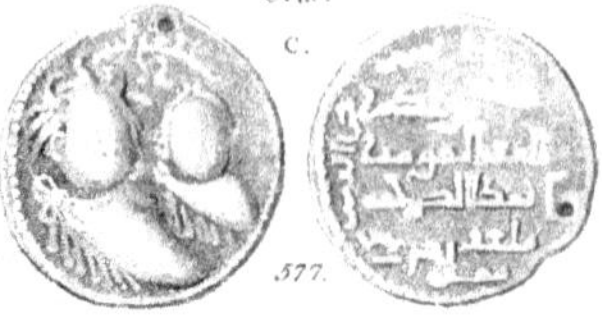

577.

CXI.
C.

572-80.

CXII.
C.

581.

Pl. III.

CXV.
C.

587.

CXX.
C.

596.

CXXIV.
C.

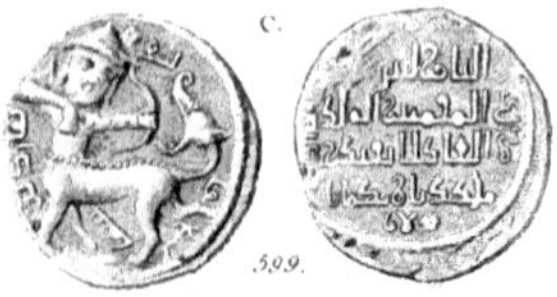

599.

CXXXI.
C.

606.

CXXXVI.
C.

610.

CXLIV.
C.

632.

Vincent Brooks Day & Son Lith.

1
4
2
3
6
5
7
8
9

URTUKIS OF KAYFA

AND KHARTAPIRT

1

2

3

5

4

6

7

8

URTUKIS OF MÁRIDÍN PL. VI.